HOMELESS PEOPLE=BUMS? NO!

A TRUE CHRISTIAN STORY

PETRA GANT

FOREWORD

For well over 10 years I ministered to the homeless. At first I did not think that I could do this kind of ministry because my heart was breaking when I saw them sleeping on the cold ground and saw them without food, but God had other plans for me.

I provided food, conversations, prayer and friendship on a weekly basis, rain or shine. I fed between 40 and 60 people each week. That created great memories and a deep bond with many of my homeless friends. In this book I am sharing my interactions with various homeless people and their stories, as well as how these encounters changed my life. I am prayerfully hoping it will change yours too.

PREFACE

My name is Petra. I was born and raised in Berlin Germany. When I was a kid, there weren't a lot of homeless people in Berlin. But I do remember whenever there was a homeless person my Mom and Dad always said "they are all bums".

I grew up in West Berlin and back then, it still had the wall. Most people lived in tall apartment buildings and so did my family. Back then, security was not as required as it is today, and we lived in a building where you just could walk into and go up the stairs to visit. Once in a blue moon I remember someone ringing our doorbell where there was a man or a woman, usually men, in front of the door stating something along the lines of "I am sorry to bother you, but I am very hungry and I was hoping that you would have a sandwich for me?" My Mom always said "yes, please wait a few minutes, I will fix you something", then she went in the kitchen and made a sandwich, while mumbling under her breath "Ah, these bums! They should all just go and work!" But then she gave away the sandwich with a smile on her face.

What I remember most were the faces of the people when they saw the sandwich. My Mom knew how to make a sandwich! Despite the fact that she seemed irritated by them, she always put a lot of love into preparing the sandwiches. She always added things that were special like BBQ sauce, or pickles.

Now, being an adult, I truly understand what people mean by 'you teach your kids with what you do, not with what you say'. As a kid I did not realize what that meant. I did hear her call the homeless 'bums' but she was kind to them and helped them whenever she could. Plus, I really had no grasp on the meaning of "bum".

I never gave homeless people a second thought; especially because of the fact that there were fewer and fewer of them. Plus being a child, anything in your little world is taken for granted.

In my mid 20s I met a US soldier, and we fell madly in love and he asked me to marry him and I said yes. Everything went very quickly. We married, had 2 kids, a boy and a girl and eventually our family moved to the US.

Alright, I am jumping forward about twenty years.

After a difficult marriage and divorcing my husband, my kids and I wound up in San Diego CA. That city has thousands of homeless people everywhere. I saw them, but really did not pay much attention to them at first.

My kids were already grown up when I encountered my very first homeless person.

This encounter started a ministry that I did for over 10 years. I remember that at first I did not think I could do this ministry – but God had other plans. I was drawn to this ministry. I kept going back. I wound up doing this every single weekend, rain or shine and I met many, MANY homeless people. Some were remarkable, some were strange, some on drugs and others heavily into alcohol, but I never judged any of them. I figured if I feel the need for a glass of wine after a long day of work – I can see why they would want that as well. Living literally on the streets must be very difficult.

I do want to share some of the things that I experienced through the years. I did not take notes as I was doing this ministry. However, I remember so much! The homeless people truly are so very dear to my heart. I realize that this is not necessarily in chronological order, but I do not think that matters much.

I am a Christian woman. Throughout my life I always went to church, prayed, read my bible, but I never actually served God. In fact, the church that I attended in Germany did not encourage people to do any type of ministry. Going to church, that is what they said was the most important thing. Well, I did not know any better at the time. I did not know what kind of plans God would have for me. In fact, I did not realize that indeed He had plans for me, plans to get involved in a ministry that is very dear to God. Now in retrospect, I realize I was what you refer to as a 'lukewarm Christian'. I was only doing the outward stuff.

But if you are a Christian, you know how God can quickly turn your world upside down. He changed everything for me and today, I am a new person. The homeless ministry was really just the beginning for me. Despite thinking that I could not do this ministry because I felt so sad, I did it anyway. God called me to it. This ministry led to other ministries that I later did. One of the ministries was a "needs" ministry. I worked for a church in Oceanside. Oceanside is a city that has very rich people and very poor people.

What this ministry did was find really poor people and once a week I met with generous folks who bought food, household goods and other supplies. We then went to the families in need and brought them everything we gathered. This ministry was very personal. I remembered my mom telling me about the time after the war. They had very little food and were depending on other people to help them survive. This ministry was not as dramatic of course. The war was long over, but when our little group brought food to the families as well as the supplies they needed, it was simply amazing!!

Another ministry that I encountered is the 'helping hands'. It was in a church that I attended at the time. I had a huge tree in my front yard and its branches were scraping across the roof. It started to cause damage to the roof. I was unable to afford a tree trimmer and being a single mother, I contacted the church. They sent two men who cut down the big branch of that tree in no time. They then cut all of it into small pieces ready for firewood. I did not have to pay for it and I found it such a blessing. I got involved in that ministry and loved it!

When I moved away, I implemented this ministry in the churches I attended. This ministry brings people in need of help, together with people who want to help. We are helping with things like rides, yard work, shopping, cleaning, moving and things of that nature. No money involved. It is very fulfilling to be able to be God's hands and feet.

But back to the homeless ministry which started everything.

My daughter was the one to bring up homeless ministry as a wonderful opportunity for us to get involved in helping other people.

Both of us wanted to do something. We wanted to help. We wanted to bring food to them. However, we were new in San Diego and did not know where to go. We did see a few people who appeared to be homeless once. It was during the day and we thought they would be at the same place at night as well. So we made about 6 sandwiches, had some water and fruit and we were heading out to that area where we saw them before. But the streets were empty.

We drove around but could not find anyone. We returned to the place where we thought they would be and simply left the bag with food there. We were counting on God to do the rest. We went home and we were disappointed. In fact we did not do anything for a long time. We felt that we needed to get to know the city better first. We needed to know where it was safe at night and where to find homeless people. Weeks went by before I actually met my first homeless person. His name was Ben.

1

B en

I worked as a consultant for an accounting software company and I traveled a lot within a 300 miles radius. One of my clients was located in National City. I went to his company on a regular basis to implement their accounting software. Such an implementation usually took about 2 – 4 months.

One of the days when I went to National City I had to stop at a red light and saw a homeless man, holding a sign stating 'will work for food, anything helps'. I did not pay much attention and wanted to continue driving. I had an appointment with my client and did not want to be late for that.

OFTEN MY WAY to clients was a long way from home and I usually dedicated the drive time to God and to prayer. When I talk to God, it is usually me who does all the talking. That morning was one of the few times when it was different. I clearly felt God telling me that I needed to give this man some money.

SOMEHOW I THOUGHT 'WHAT? NO!' I did not want to give my money away. I was wondering if this is 'really God' who is pushing me to do this. Then I remembered a time at church when I talked to one of my pastors. He told me "the way you'll know that something comes from God is when it lines up with the bible. Often it is something that is something that will be out of our comfort zone".

THIS WAS one of those times! In the bible God clearly tells us to 'feed my sheep', so I knew I needed to listen and give this guy some money. I pulled over to check my purse. All I had was a $10 bill. I drove up to the man, stretched out my hand and handed him the money. "Here, this is for you" I stated. He looked at me and smiled just a little faint smile and reached for the money.   There was that moment when both he and I had our hands on the money, as he said to me "Thank you Ma'am, may God bless you." I let go of the money and grabbed his hand and I responded "Thanks, and may God bless YOU". He looked at my hand in disbelief, then looked into my eyes and asked "you are touching me?" I just nodded and smiled. Then I saw tears in his eyes as he said "No one has touched me in 15 years!"

Nοτ ηαvιng any contact with anyone for 15 years? Not being touched at all by anyone? I thought my heart would break. I turned off the engine of and got out of my car to give him a big hug.

We stood there in this embrace for at least 10 - 15 minutes, both of us sobbing. I had no idea what he might be thinking, but he held me tight. I returned his hug. I could feel his body trembling, and I could feel his tears on my shoulder. I did not expect that this moment would forever change my life.

I ςαLLεD my client to let him know that I would be late that morning. Ben and I sat down and talked. Honestly, I do not remember much of what we were talking about. I do remember Ben's eyes – they seemed to be illuminated from within. He was doing most of the talking and I remember my parents and many other people always calling homeless people bums. I realized that he was not a bum! He was a man that had fallen on hard times, a man who was lonely and who was starving for conversation and attention. Starving for human contact and just a few moments of being a person who is not homeless, but who is a man who needed to just talk. I spent about an hour with him when I told him that I needed to get to work. We hugged again and I promised I would stop by the next time. His eyes immediately were overshadowed with sadness again. I do not think he believed that I would come back as I promised.

WHEN I GOT HOME that evening, I kept thinking about Ben. I was wondering where he lived, whether he has some sort of place in which to live, I kept thinking about him and wondered if I would see him again.

JUST A FEW DAYS LATER, I went to that client again. I had made a couple of sandwiches, just the way my Mom used to make them with meat and cheese, a little BBQ sauce and a lot of love. Plus I had a bottle of water, some fruit and a couple of hard boiled eggs.

. . .

I CAME to the corner where I met him, but I did not see him. I felt great disappointment. I looked around for him and there he was, just down the street. He was sitting with his sign "will work for food, anything helps" I drove up to him and when I slowed down, he looked up. His eyes seemed to just light up. He was glad to see me. He was waiving to me as I parked the car and I waived back.

BEN WAS TOUCHED by the fact that I really did stop by to see him and he loved the food. The way he looked at the sandwich, reminded me of the homeless people in my childhood. There was the same light in his eyes. I stayed a little while and we talked a little. Again it was him who did most of the talking. All I did was asking him how his day was, and he told me all about his day.

I STOPPED to see him every time I worked in National City. One day he told me that there was another man who has not eaten in days; so he asked me if it was OK if he would share his food with him. Yes, of course! I told him that I would bring food for both of them from now on. Soon there were 10 meals that I brought with me. And yes, my homeless ministry was born.

2

Church without walls

I ATTENDED the Rock Church at that time. It is a mega church and they have many ministries, I want to say 60 – maybe 80 ministries. I had not really paid much attention to that, but one day when I was looking at the bulletin I saw that there is an event called 'church without walls' and read on. It was a ministry to homeless people! What it was all about was a bunch of loving people who got together every Saturday morning in Balboa Park, which was nearby. There were a couple of pastors, a few musicians and singers, plus group of people who prepared food and juices, cakes, cookies and fruit. Wow, I thought I found the perfect ministry for me! I wrote down the address and time and I decided I would be there that next Saturday.

W_{HEN} I _{ARRIVED} there that following Saturday, I could not believe my eyes. So many homeless people! Men, women and kids! Kids!! I never even thought about kids being homeless before! I felt that lump in my throat and tears in my eyes. This was the first time when I thought 'I can't do this' and walked the other way, but I had to go back. I had to at least see what this is about so I could tell Ben and his friends about this place.

W_{ELL}, I sat under a tree to watch. A young pastor gave a very encouraging message. He talked about the love of God and how God loves everyone. A few bibles were placed on one of the tables and people could borrow one if they wanted to. Then the musicians sang worship songs and people were singing along. I looked around and the amount of homeless people had doubled! There were about 170 – 200 people. Again I thought that I cannot do this! I felt totally overwhelmed. I did look around and I saw their eyes lifted up, some of them had raised their hands as they were worshiping, and others had their eyes closed. It was so nice to see, yet it was surprising to me. I thought that it was amazing, these people had nothing! Yet they were here to praise God. I really felt blessed to be a part of this.

As the worship team was singing I could smell the food being prepared. It smelled wonderful. I looked over and I saw meatloaf, veggies, potatoes, rolls and bread, cookies and coffee and tea, water and juice and fresh fruit as well. One of the pastors said a prayer over the food and invited everyone to come and get some free food.

The homeless people built a long line and each of them not only received a hot meal for that moment, but also a to-go bag with fruit and cookies and a sandwich as well. My heart was melting when I saw this. So many homeless people were fed that day with two meals each. All the volunteers were smiling and said nice things to them, served them and just loved them. It was remarkable.

But again, I looked and saw all these homeless people! People who do not have a place to call home! People who sleep somewhere on the street! If they were lucky, they were able to find a place that had some sort of roof – in case it rained. People that were hungry most of the time! My heart was breaking! No way can I do this, I thought as I was walking over to one of the volunteers.

I HEARD myself asking "what kinds of things do the volunteers do here?" The guy smiled at me and told me that I could help cook, serve food, clean up, pray with the homeless, just spend time with them because they do not have a lot of people speak to them and everyone needs that. I could also help with the worship team, hand out the song lyrics. There is always plenty to do. I felt my body trembling; again I just knew I could not do any of this because my heart was breaking. I thanked the guy and started to walk away.

I TURNED around for a final glance and tears ran down my face. I felt such sorrow to see all these people. Hungry, lonely, unprotected from the elements and only God knows what else. I drove home thinking about these homeless people. I kept seeing them and their kids. KIDS! I was wondering if any of them would go to a shelter. Are they all living on the street? Do they eat every day? My thoughts were just running through my head not really comprehending all the things that were going on. I just knew that I felt greatly for them. When I arrived at home, I sat down and I cried. I was so touched by what I had seen. I could not get over it. I told my daughter about it and she was telling me that the church has a homeless ministry as well. They all meet on Monday evening. Everyone brings something to eat and then they go and feed the homeless downtown. – Why did I not know this? Oh it did not matter I knew now. Just wait until Monday.

3

*D*owntown

THE NEXT MONDAY at 6 PM I went to the meeting place on 3rd Avenue, a small parking lot. When I got there I was surprised. There were only a handful of people there. I expected a lot of people because the Rock church has thousands of people attending any of the 6 services that they had at the time. I waited in my car for a little while, thinking this may not be the right group. I had made 30 sandwiches along with some bottled water. I left that in the car and went to the group to see if they were from the Rock. Yes they were. We introduced each other. Mostly very young people with a big heart for Jesus and they were ready to go out there and pray with the homeless people. Only two other people had brought food.

We built a circle and one man, Richard, prayed a prayer of protection and God's wisdom for us. This was actually an amazing experience! We all held hands and somehow there was an immediate bond that seemed tangible! All of us had the welfare of homeless people at heart. Having food or not – we all wanted to help them. These prayers we prayed every week prior to going to serve the homeless were truly powerful each and every time.

After the prayer, everyone put the food they had brought with them in the middle and Richard and one other guy shared it amongst us. I had 2 of the sandwiches that I brought and an apple.

We went to the next block over and there was a big square with a really big parking lot in the middle, surrounded by streets and office buildings. This was a very busy part of town. During the day all the big buildings were crowded with people who went to work, meetings and just business events. But towards the evening there were less and less people around. When it started to get dark, a lot of homeless people came and brought their stuff with them. Here is where between 50 and 80 people made their place for the night. I had my two sandwiches and I went to talk to one of the homeless people. "Are you hungry? Would you like to have a sandwich?" that became my opening line. The answer was almost always 'yes'. It was a great way to get a conversation started.

MOST OF THE time they were sitting on the street, some of them had sleeping bags or blankets, others had cardboard or nothing at all. I usually began a conversation by asking things like how are you doing, or how was your day? The first couple of times I felt awkward, but I learned very quickly that most of the homeless people were all too eager to talk and tell me all about their day. Often I'd ask if I can sit with them. They usually loved that. I have to admit that I loved it as well. It felt like a couple of friends just sitting and chatting. I enjoyed the talks that I had with them. I usually am very bad with remembering names, but doing this ministry it was somehow different. I think God got involved and allowed me to remember all their names; it was something that meant a lot to them. I did not know that at the beginning, but God certainly did. I say that because I remembered their names right away and still know them all today.

. . .

I MET Felix at the square. He was my height, had long brown wavy hair and no teeth in his mouth, but he always had the biggest brightest smile that you can imagine. He always loved to receive some food and he always asked for prayer. Every time I saw him, he had some sort of joke to tell. The other thing he always did, was ask me how my back felt, because the first time I met him, I had done something to my back and it was hurting. He asked permission to massage my back for me. The first time he asked that I had "oh no way" right on my lips, but when I looked into his eyes, I saw such a caring loving look in them that I heard myself say "yes that would be nice" He did massage my shoulders and my back and it made my back feel better. Then he said to me "it is just a small way of saying thank you for the food and the company". That warmed my heart.

I SAW Felix every time I did this ministry. I have never ever seen him in a bad mood, except for one day. He sat at his usual spot and the first thing I noticed was that he was barefoot. I went to him offered some food and asked him how his day was. He looked up to me and said that he had fallen asleep and someone took all his stuff, including his shoes. He had tears in his eyes. I could hardly believe my ears! Who would take stuff from a homeless person?? How cold-hearted do you have to be to do such a thing? Felix started to tell me that this happens a lot. "As a homeless person you have to have all your things with you at all times, otherwise some other homeless person will take it from you. They may either need it for themselves, or they will sell it to another homeless person." My heart went out to him. The next day, after telling my daughter all about what happened to Felix, she and I went to the store, bought a backpack, a sleeping bag and some shoes for him. I remember I made a special trip to bring him those things. Usually I only went downtown on Mondays, but this was different. He had no shoes and no supplies. When he saw me he smiled big and said "what now, is it already Monday again?" I told him "No, I came here today to bring you a couple of things, things that could not wait until next week." and returned his smile. Then I got everything out of the big plastic bag. His eyes got big as he looked at all the things and he asked "This is not a joke? This is really all for me?" "Yup, it is all for you my friend!" I assured him. He inspected everything, told me that the backpack was perfect, and bigger than his old one. Then he realized the shoes were exactly his size. I handed him a pair of new socks, and he put both socks and shoes on his feet. He wrapped his arms around me and hugged me so hard; he had tears in his eyes. At the same time he was also smiling from ear to ear. Again I have to say, the 'little' things we take for granted, shoes, clothes, safety –is not a normal thing for the homeless. It is a daily struggle. I still remember Felix's eyes. They got big when I told him that these things were for him. He was so happy. It really blessed me.

B etty

 Saturday was coming around and I was debating whether or not I wanted to go back to Balboa Park to Church without Walls. I remembered all too well how overwhelming it was to me to see so many homeless families. What would I do? How would I help? There was a big part of me that did not want to go. But when Saturday came around, I got up and drove out there.

I went over to the ministry table and asked how I could help. I was told to just find a homeless person and sit with them. I slowly walked around to see if I could find someone that was alone. Lots of the volunteers were already talking to homeless people. There were also smaller and bigger groups of people that sat together and talked. I did not feel comfortable sitting with a group; this was all so new to me. It was so very different from the square. But then I saw a lady. She was heavyset and sat on the grass. She was intently looking at her feet. She sat on a beach towel under a big tree in the shade. Her black curly hair was short and it looked like it had not been combed in a while. I approached her and asked her how she was doing. She looked up at me and said she was fine. I asked if it was OK for me to sit with her and she said yes. We introduced ourselves and began to chat. Betty and I made small talk about the weather, Balboa Park, sunshine and things like that. But then Betty turned serious. She shared with me that she had nowhere to go and that her health was failing. Her voice was strong as she spoke, but tears were running down her face. I grabbed her hand and held it while she spoke. Then she asked me if I would pray for her.

I know I mentioned previously that prayer was something that was a big part of the ministry, but coming to Balboa Park was really the first time when a homeless person asked me to pray for them. I looked at Betty and I said of course. I folded my hands, closed my eyes and began to silently pray for her. About 20 -30 seconds later I felt her hit me on my arm and she said "Hey!! Out loud!!!"

I stopped and looked at her. My thoughts were racing. I had never really prayed for anyone out loud before. Don't get me wrong, I prayed a lot, but in silence. Here she was, her big brown eyes locked with mine, her head tilted to the side. "I want to hear what you say to God" she demanded.

I grabbed both of her hands instead of folding mine, smiled, cleared my throat and began praying out loud. It only took a few seconds and I felt at ease. I realized, I was talking to God and He knows my heart. He put His calmness into me and I prayed for Betty's situation, prayed for her protection and her health.

When I was done, I opened my eyes and there she was, just sobbing. Her tears were just running down her cheeks. She let go of my hands and pulled me into a big hug. She kept saying "thank you, thank you, thank you sister."

We sat together during the worship and the mini sermon. Then she went in line to get her food. I went over to the food table and helped handing out the food. After that I went home, I felt so very blessed! My heart was filled with joy. Then I started thinking of Ben. When I first met him, how he touched my heart with his need for human contact. Here were dozens of homeless people who had the very same need. Yes, not only did I know that I could do this ministry after all, but I felt that I had to! I felt that I could make a difference, even if it was only a small difference, but I knew that it was important to give it my best.

Chapter Five Richard and David

One Saturday, I went shopping for the homeless

ministry. I bought bread and mayo, ham, Salami and cheese and a big bottle of BBQ sauce. Also, I purchased juices and oranges to feed 40 people. I wanted to have more food this time.

When we arrived that next Monday evening, there were a few more people there. Richard was already collecting the food and waters from everyone. I gave him 30 of the sandwiches and waters but held back 10 of them for my daughter and me to hand out.

I saw Richard talking to a new person, a man named David. Richard introduced him to me and my daughter. He told us that David had been in jail for a couple of years for drug related issues. He now was free to go home, only his family did not want him to come back. So, David was homeless, but he wanted to help with this ministry. I liked that!

Richard was coming over to me and he asked me if I would save one of the sandwiches for David. I told him that it would be my pleasure. Then he asked if he could also have one. I looked at him and did not really know what to say. After all, these sandwiches were for the homeless! He smiled and said "you may not know this Petra, but I am homeless too."

This was one of those moments where I was so grateful that I did not say what I was thinking. I was grateful that I had kept my mouth shut. "I did not know you are homeless Richard!!" He responded "It is not the kind of thing that I usually talk about." I did take two of the sandwiches and put them aside. We then headed out to the square together and handed out food, prayer and companionship.

I saw Richard sitting with some of the homeless people and I found myself watching him. He was a tall guy maybe 6'3" thin build, a long gray beard and long hair held together in a ponytail. I did not realize that he was homeless. Then again, lots of the homeless people do not look like they are. I just admired him for running this ministry!

Much later I learned that he was going to the Rock church on a regular basis. Plus, he had been one of the leaders in this ministry for a long time. It really touched my heart. Someone who is homeless himself, is leading a homeless ministry. I was truly impressed by that. Now that I knew that both Richard and David were homeless, I always made extra food for them.

I did this Monday evening ministry for many months; in fact, it was about a year or so when I got really tired of the fact that most of the time I was the only one to bring real food. It was always divided up and I felt that I never had enough food to hand out. Even today I am wondering if I was selfish feeling that way. But there was that one day when only 5 people showed up on Monday evening to do the ministry. Someone outright asked me "what did you bring for us to hand out to the homeless today?" That shocked me just a bit. I had made 50 sandwiches, so each of us got

10. We went to the square and there were a lot of homeless out there. I saw Felix and we were talking for maybe 2 minutes when one of the volunteers came to me and asked "can I have some more sandwiches, I handed mine all out." I swallowed hard because that was just not right. I looked at her and said "handing out the sandwiches is nice, but it is supposed to be an opening to talk to them and give them some company!" She leaned towards me and whispered "They smell bad; I do not want to get too close to them."

It took all of me not to yell at her, but that was one of the factors that made me decide that I would do this ministry on my own from now on. Today I know that I was selfish. I should have shared and I should have taught the volunteers how to use the food as an opening to talk to them, to pray for them and to offer them respect and friendship, Instead of judging how they acted. But I was still a baby Christian when it came to serving God. I made the food and I wanted to hand it out myself. After all, that was the best part – seeing the homeless happy, even if it was just for a little while. Enjoy their smiles, their stories about their day; give them company, conversation, prayers and food.

O n my own

M<small>ONDAYS WERE ALWAYS</small> a bit stressful for me because I was working. By the time I got home, I had to hurry up so much to get there on time. My new plan would work out much better for me. From now on my weekends were consumed by this ministry, and the meals that I prepared from that day on were not just sandwiches.

Saturdays I went to Costco to shop for all the groceries that I needed. The meals were something like this: potato salad, BBQ meatballs, juice, a banana or other soft fruit and some hardboiled eggs. I made a variety of salads and it was not always meatballs, I'd bring chicken drumsticks, hot dogs and things like that.

During the cooler months I cooked soups like chicken noodle, chili, bean soup and many other warm meals.

When my shopping was done, I started to prepare for Sunday. I made the salad already and put them in small individual containers and put them in the fridge. Then I prepared the brown bags with juice or water, the fruit, a granola bar and a napkin along with plastic utensils and tiny one-use bags with salt and pepper.

Sunday morning, I went to church and when I came home, I had a couple of hours to myself. Finally, I prepared the warm food. Whatever food I made, I wrapped it in foil paper; enough food for one person at a time. I had a large Styrofoam box which I lined with foil paper. It made for the perfect container to keep food warm. Then I loaded up my car and I went out to the square on Sunday night.

I was pleasantly surprised how much nicer it was to do this by myself! No time limits and I could truly devote time to all the new friends I made. Many of the homeless were the same people as on Monday night, but there were others that I had never seen before. Daniel was one of them. He had his space a little away from everyone else. He stayed in front of a house that had a garage with a large overhang that kept the rain away.

San Diego does not see a whole lot of rain, but if you actually sleep on the street, you will get drenched if it does rain. Most homeless did not have the 'luxury' of having an overhang or roof of sorts. They had to go elsewhere to keep dry, like a bridge or freeway overpass. Daniel told me that the owner of the house had asked him to stay if he promised to keep everything clean and keep trouble away. Daniel smiled a big smile when he told me "I can handle that!"

I spent lots of time with Daniel. We talked about all kinds of topics and we both enjoyed the conversations we had. Often his buddy Paul chimed in as well. Paul and Daniel shared the same spot every night and they were friends. Paul was the quieter one between the two. He mostly liked to listen. Daniel was usually waiting for me on Sunday evening. I arrived there around the same time every weekend. He also made sure to have a parking spot available. I am not sure how he did that, but I had the same parking spot every time. This ministry had blossomed to an outreach food ministry! I had a cart like many of the homeless had, where I put my food and water and I pushed it around to bring the food to everyone. Often Daniel actually came and walked with me and helped me hand out the food. It did not take very long before I knew just about everyone there and they were looking forward to seeing me on Sunday evenings.

Chapter Seven Bibles

I also still went to Church without Walls. I did not go every Saturday, but at least once a month. One of the things that I noticed was that most of the homeless did not have their own bibles and although the volunteers brought a few bibles that they could borrow for the morning, they ran out every time. So, I decided I would buy a bunch of bibles, which I quickly realized I could not afford. Bibles are not cheap. So, I called wholesalers hoping that they would sell me bibles cheaper. I had to make many calls before I finally got lucky. I found a wholesaler who was a Christian and he loved my story. He sold me bibles at $1 per bible, but I had to buy 200 minimum. That was OK with me. I bought 300 bibles and another 100 in Spanish. It was a lot of money, but I had prayed about this and felt it was the right thing to do. I could hardly wait to get them.

When they finally arrived, I prayed over those bibles and I felt God telling me that I need to write a few personal lines into each of them before handing them out. So I sat and waited for God to tell me what to write. He gave me the following bible verses:

Hebrews 4:16 So let us come boldly to the throne of our gracious God. There we will receive His mercy and we will find grace to help us when we need it most.

Hebrews 13:5,6 Don't love money; be satisfied with what you have . For God has said, I will never fail you. I will never abandon you.

1st Peter 5:6,7 So humble yourselves under the mighty power of God and at the right time He will lift you up in honor. Give Him all your worries and cares to God, for He cares about you.

1st Corinthians 15:57, 58 But thank God for He gives us victory over sin and death through our Lord Jesus Christ. Therefore my dear brothers and sisters, be strong and immovable. Always work enthusiastically for the Lord, for you know that nothing you do for the Lord is ever useless.

I typed those passages up and highlighted them in each and every bible. Then I hand-wrote something personal in each bible; it was something unique for each one. I prayed about that and I waited for God to tell me what to write. I also worked with a friend of mine who speaks Spanish and she translated the sayings for me.

I took all of the bibles with me and handed them out at Church without Walls. As the homeless were in line for food, I walked with my big bag of bibles and handed them to anyone who wanted one. Most people took one. Some said they already have one. Some simply refused, but it was such a blessing to me to hand out God's word to those who wanted it. In fact, there were so many bibles to hand out that it took three Saturdays to hand them all out. I only had a handful of them left after that. It was such a good feeling to see all the people having their own bible. It was heartwarming to see some of them read in the bible that they had received. I just loved it. I prayed quietly and thanked God for allowing me to see how much they enjoyed their own bible.

That Saturday I went home feeling great joy. I felt that God loved what happened that day. I loved it too.

When I came home that day, I told my daughter about it and she listened very closely. Then she said to me "Mom, you are making an eternal difference!" I did not think about that. In fact, this was not my reason for doing it at all. I just wanted to make them happy. But my daughter assured me that handing out hundreds of bibles will have eternal ripple effects. She told me that one day when I am going to heaven, I will see all of those people there and many of them will be there because I gave them a bible and lead them to Christ. Well, OK I thought, that would a bonus.

R ubin

T_HE FOLLOWING_ day I went to the square. I remember that I had made Chinese noodles for the homeless that day. I do remember that because that particular Sunday turned out to be very special indeed. I had the left-over bibles with me as well. I thought there will be someone out there who will love to have their own bible.

M_Y USUAL PARKING_ space was available and I stopped by to see Daniel. We talked a little bit but I told him I will come by when all the hot food was handed out. He said he could help me with handing out the food and I took him up on that. I had a lot of food with me and the help was very welcomed. Plus, I have to be honest – I just loved it when the homeless people, who need so much help themselves, would help me. It meant something to them. They felt needed and wanted. And it meant so much to me, because I got to be a small part of making them feel that way.

AFTER HANDING out more than half of the food, we approached a woman who sat on the street. I asked if she was hungry and if she would like some food. Yes! She wanted food. I also told her that I had bibles and if she would like one. She told me she had one already.

NEXT TO HER was someone all covered up with a large blanket, seemingly asleep. Our conversation caused him to toss the blanket aside and he sat up and looked at me stating "It is you!! IT IS YOU!!!" I was not sure that I knew him and was not sure what was going on, but I said "It is me" and I smiled. He began to cry. I knelt down next to him and grabbed his shoulder. I was really not sure what to say but I mumbled "I am sorry, how can I help?" He looked up at me, his face wet with tears. He was sobbing. I mean really sobbing. It took a little bit before he was able to speak. "Yesterday, I was so sick of it. I was sick of everything! I told myself that I am going to end it all. Today was the day. But then I thought I should have one last good meal. I went to Church without Walls. They always have good food there. And then there you were! You gave me a bible. You gave it to me and said that God loved me. I just laughed but took it." I did remember him now. He did laugh, it was a dismissive laugh, but he took the bible. I also remember that I prayed a silent prayer that he may read the bible, even if it is just a few verses. I prayed that God would show up in a mighty way. "I remember you now!" I told him. He continued. "I did not look at the bible – it was just a bible. I got my food and ate but then I opened the bible anyway. There was this hand-written note!" He began to cry again. He grabbed his bible and handed it to me. I opened it and it said, 'Tomorrow is a new day and a new day is a new beginning'. Now I felt tears in my eyes. I looked at him. He asked if he could have a hug. Oh yes, I hugged him. I could feel him still crying. After a while I heard him whisper "thank you, thank you so much. I wanted to kill myself yesterday. You, the bible, this little message changed my mind." I was thinking about the time I wrote little messages in those bibles. I prayed that God would give me the words to write and that God would make sure that the bible with the right message would be received by someone who needs it. I felt so close to God that moment. He is in the details! He made sure that this bible got into the right hands, at the right moment. God saved his life! He used me as His tool. I felt honored and humbled at the same time. Even now, after all these years, I get tears in my eyes as I am typing this. He told me his name was Rubin and we talked.

DANIEL CLEARED his throat and I looked at him. He offered to just hand out the food alone while I sat here with my new friend. I gladly took him up on that. Rubin told me about his life. He had a wife and a nice place where they lived. Pretty much a perfect life, he called it. He had a job that was not too great, but it paid the bills. Then there was a car accident. A drunk driver hit him so hard that most of his bones were broken and he had all kinds of internal injuries. He was in the hospital for many months. His job was gone and shortly thereafter the insurance ran out. His wife did not want to deal with this and left him and took all their stuff with her. So, when he was released from the hospital, he had nothing and no-one. He was on the street. He fell into a deep depression and stayed on the street. Everything seemed useless and worthless to him. And eventually he decided to die.

WE SAT and talked for a couple of hours. I asked him what he was going to do now. He told me that he has a brother in Seattle and he would catch a bus or train and get there. Later I prayed for him, a long heartfelt prayer. We hugged good bye and I never saw Rubin again. But Daniel told me that he had almost all the money for the bus but there were a couple of homeless guys who gave him the additional cash he needed. So, Rubin went to see his brother. I still pray for him now and then. I am counting on God to have cleared the way for Rubin.

D ee

ONE EVENING when I was at the square, I met a man who sat in a corner leaning against a building and he looked soooo sad. I approached him and said hello. He did not even look up and said;" What do you want?" I replied "Oh, I want nothing, but I do have some food, if you are hungry you can have some. " Again, he was not looking up but said "I am tired of days old bread. I am not hungry for that." My response was "well, if you are not hungry, I understand, but I have some chicken drum sticks and home-made pasta salad. Plus, some juice and an orange and a granola bar." As I was talking, he started to look at me and his face changed and showed some excitement. Yeah, he took that food. He thanked me. I saw such sadness in his eyes. I asked him if I could pray for him. "Oh no, that is useless anyway. No God worth a damn is going to give a sh... um, is not going to care about me." So, I asked again – I would like to pray anyway – for what do you need prayer? "He shook his head, looked at me and said "you can pray if you want, but I do not need prayer. You know nothing about me why pray for me?"

I DID NOT RESPOND and prior to praying for him, I asked God to give me the words, because this guy was right, I knew nothing about him. I asked for his name, he told me that his name is Dee. He actually stood up. He was tall – about 6'4" or so. He was roughly in his early to mid-50's. He was a handsome black man who's face showed that he had some rough times in his life. I grabbed his hands and began to pray. I do not remember exactly what I prayed for in the beginning. Something along the lines of safety, God's care and comfort and all of a sudden I started praying for his health, for his stomach. I prayed that God may heal his stomach, prayed that God would help him to eat well and to heal his body. I asked God that He would supply the right food for him. I actually remember praying for quite a while for him. When I finished, I looked up to him and there were tears. He quickly wiped them away.

Then he looked at me and rather skeptical he asked me "Who told you? Who did you talk to?" I did not know what he meant so I asked "I do not understand." "My stomach!" he responded, "how did you know?" I smiled and then I told him that I always ask God how to pray – and He gave me the words. Dee did not want to believe me and sat back down opened the food and said" thanks for this – take care"

I took that as my queue and left.

THE NEXT TIME I saw Dee was several weeks later also down-town, but at a different corner. I recognized him and walked toward him. "Hi Dee, how are you? How is your stomach", I asked. He looked, smiled a big smile and said "You remembered my name!" I smiled and said yes. I usually was forgetful when it comes to names but like I said before, God is in the details, and I suppose He knows that it is important to the homeless that someone remembers their name – that someone cares. "So how is your stomach?" I asked him. To my surprise he said" There is no change, but if you want to pray some more, that would be nice." I was fighting tears. This was amazing to me! Yes, I prayed for him. For his stomach, safety and God again gave me words to pray for – I prayed for his family. His brother, I prayed that Dee would reach out to him. When I was done praying Dee laughed out loud. "No seriously lady, you are talking to someone! How did you know that I have a brother? "I looked at him and told him that I did not know, but God revealed to me that this is what I needed to pray for."

WE WOUND up talking for about an hour or so. He told me about his brother, whom he had not spoken to in many years. His brother and Dee had a falling out and his brother did not even know that Dee was homeless. I wanted to talk him into contacting his brother, but I was quiet and prayed about it instead.

AS WE WERE TALKING one homeless woman came over. She looked in bad shape. Her hair looked very much neglected and her clothes were torn. She came and yelled at me "why are you coming here bitch? Go away! No-one wants you here! You are from the devil! Get out of here!" Her face was angry looking. I did not answer her. Dee got up and told her "Girl, go away, this lady is not of the devil. She is a good person who brings us food. He offered her the food that I had given to him. She took it and laughed at me. She started to sing a song and walked away. I just looked at Dee and he explained that she is mentally not right. He told me that she walks the streets and screams at people all the time. Dee told me her name was Pam. I gave Dee some more food since he gave his to Pam. Then I was heading home. It was late. As I walked away, I turned around. I saw Dee getting a blanket from his backpack and he waved goodbye. I waved back at him.

W_{HEN} I _{GOT HOME}, I walked through my house. I had a 3 bedroom home, a fenced in back yard. I looked at all the little knick-knacks that I had all over the place. Cards and pictures on display, books on the shelf, a couple of TV's, sofa, table, beds, a kitchen with a fridge full of food, a bathroom with a nice tub and a shower, heat and air conditioning. I thought of Dee, Rubin, Richard and David and I began to cry. I felt like all the stuff that I had, was "stuffocating" me. Here I was in a cozy place with enough stuff to fill up someone else's home as well. Each of the homeless people would be happy if they could sleep on the floor in my house. Have a night in safety. I cried. I felt helpless. I wanted to do so much more but realized that I cannot do every-thing. But I cried a long good cry.

8

Heart Problems

This book is not about me, it is about my homeless friends. But I am going to share some of my personal life as well, because it is very important to the relationship I had with my homeless friends.

When I was a teenager, I began having issues with my heart. For no apparent reason, my heart started racing up to 250 beats per minute. Just for a little while, and then just as quickly as it started, it would snap back to normal rhythm. No, it did not slow down, but just stopped racing. I told my mom about it and we went to the doctor. He checked me out but could not really do anything. He said to come back when the heart is racing. Well, that was difficult because it did not happen that often and when it did, it was sudden, only lasted a minute or two – never enough to go to the doctor. So, I simply lived with it.

As THE YEARS WENT BY, these heart rhythms changed. It slowly started to last longer and happened more often. I was given a Holster Monitor that I wore for 48 hours to catch this rapid heartbeat. By the grace of God, I had an episode of the rapid heartbeat while wearing the Holster Monitor, so it was recorded. The doctors analyzed it and gave me some pills to regulate the heartbeat, but it did not work.

Without too much detail – the long and short of it was that they wanted to give me all kinds of drugs but I did not want to take all kinds of pills without knowing that they would help. I did not want to be a guinea pig.

OVER THE YEARS this condition got worse and worse. It happened much more often and often lasted 30 minutes or more. There were a couple of times when my heart was racing while doing my ministry. I usually would not let it show. I just kept doing my thing and maybe left earlier than usual. Simply because when my heart was beating so fast for a longer period of time, I felt exhausted by the time it went back to normal.

ONE DAY, as I was driving to work, my heart started to race again. So I turned around and went back home. I wanted to lie down. Often that helped. When I got home, my daughter was still there. She clearly was worried about me. But I assured her that I would be fine and she could go to work. She did. I stayed home that day. My heart was racing for several hours and I called my daughter and she came home to take me to the hospital.

THE DOCTORS WORKED on me and checked everything out. They brought in a crash cart; I knew what it was because I had seen it in movies. Then the doctor told me that they will give me medicine that will stop my heart and "usually" the heart starts up by itself again. In case it does not, here is the crash cart.

"NO!!!" I almost screamed that "I know my heart is racing, but it is beating and I like that! I do not want that medicine!" Yes, now I was actually scared.

MY DAUGHTER HAD CALLED my son and he now was also there. They both supported my decision to not take that medicine. My daughter prayed over me and shortly thereafter my heart snapped back to normal again. But now – now they had plenty of EKG data to work with. I made an appointment to see a specialist.

W_{HEN THE DAY} came and I went to see the doctor, he took time to truly explain what was going on with my heart. He told me that every healthy heart has four "feelers" that control the electric pulses that make the heart beat. Me, instead of four feelers, I had FIFTEEN of them. That is what made my heart go crazy. He told me that over the years the heart grew more and more of them. Hmm, OK! Now that we know this, what can be done?

H_{E EXPLAINED} the procedure to me "We will go through your groin area, through the veins up to and into your heart. With a special tool we will get inside the heart and burn away the extra feelers. "He said that and smiled at me. It took me just a moment to really process this. He wanted to go inside my heart with a tool and BURN things away, things that were growing inside my heart. I started to feel a little queasy. I told him that I do not like that idea. He assured me that this is the only procedure that would take care of what is going on. I asked for time to think about it.

. . .

I SHARED all this with my kids and we discussed it as a family. They said to me that they would support whatever I wanted to do. So, the decision was mine. I thought about it for a few days and finally prayed about it. After praying about it I realized that there would only be three possible outcomes. One, I would not do this and would have to deal with it for the rest of my life – not an option!!

Two I would do it, wake up and never have to deal with this again – sounds good.

Three – I would do this and not wake up, I would die.

Well, I see that either I get well, or I will go home. Either way is well with me.

I DECIDED TO DO IT, but it was several weeks before this could actually happen.

9

Sharing the news

THE NEXT TIME I went to feed the homeless, I shared with Daniel what was going on. He sat still and listened to me. When I finished, he grabbed my hands and started to pray. I never heard him pray before. His words were simple but straight forward. He asked God "fix her God. Make the doctor do a good job. Make sure that the doctor sleeps well the night before and don't let his hands be all shaky. Just fix her God. We all love her here."

I was in tears. There is nothing more humbling than a homeless person praying for you. We hugged.

This meant so much to me! I asked him not to share this information. It was pretty personal. He smiled at me, there was no answer, no more talking, just a big smile.

As the weeks went by, Daniel asked me questions about my health. He wanted to know what hospital I was going to and if the doctor had done this procedure before. He asked what day and time the procedure would take place so he could pray for me. I was so touched and told him that it was to be on Monday at 8 AM first thing in the morning. He was worried about me because I started to be nervous about all of this. He kept telling me that he would pray for me. Then he got serious and said he had to tell me something and he is hoping I would not be angry. What?? "Petra, you wanted me not to talk about this, but there are so many of us who love you so much. I did share it with some of the others. We are all praying for you regularly. We usually do not hang out together, but we met and we prayed for you. I hope you are not mad."

How could I be??? I had tears in my eyes. This really touched me deeply. I had been doing this ministry for a few years at this point and lots of the people there knew me and I knew them. We regularly talked about things that mattered to them. I never really shared much about me because this was not about me. I never really thought about the fact that they could care so much about me. I shared that with Daniel and he smiled. "Yeah, at first it was the food you brought, but you are a real friend to all of us." he said and smiled – well, how could I be mad. I really appreciated the love.

During the following weeks I kept going to see them and bring food. And I answered all the questions they had. It was like a new thing that made the bond we had formed over the years even closer. I shared that with both of my kids and my son was rather quiet. He did not like it that I went every weekend all by myself to feed homeless people. Often, I stayed out until 9 PM or 10 PM and he worried about me. I often invited him to come with me some time. My daughter also encouraged him to come along. But he just shook his head, telling me that this was not his thing.

But of course, that never stopped me from bragging about both of my kids. My son, a US Marine, larger than life in his 6'8" body, has always been difficult to overlook. He is a strong man who is very protective of his family. It was easy to brag about him as well as my daughter. She came with me often, so she knew what it meant to be there for them.

I remember praying the night before my procedure. I was asking God to take care of my kids and also of the homeless in case He was calling me home.

Chapter Twelve Hospital

I do not remember for sure, whether my appointment was on a Thursday or a Friday. The weekend prior to my procedure, I told my homeless friends that I would not be there next week. They all assured me that they would miss me and that they would pray for me. I loved that. It is difficult to put into words how very humbling it is to be loved by homeless people.

The day of my procedure my son came to my house to take me to the hospital. Both of my kids came with me. I have to be honest, I was extremely nervous. We arrived about 30 minutes early – we were supposed to do that for paperwork. Walking through the halls made my heart beat faster. No, it was not racing, but it was beating faster and seemingly harder. I filled out some paperwork and then we we headed to a waiting area. As we turned around the corner there was Daniel! Daniel and Paul were sitting in the waiting room and their eyes got big when they saw me walking in. They smiled and so did I. My daughter knew them and I finally had a chance to introduce my son to two of my homeless friends. The two guys gave me big hugs. "How did you get here?" I wanted to know because I realized that the square was about 18 – 20 miles away from the hospital. Paul smiled and said "we walked. We left very early this morning". Daniel added "We just wanted to come here to pray for you and bring you this." He handed over a get well card. It was signed by about 45 of my homeless friends. Well wishes, prayers, good thoughts, just greetings and expressions of their love. Tears were rolling. I thanked them both.

The nurse stuck her face in the room and called me in. David grabbed my hand and said a 4 word prayer;" God, watch over her" I hugged them both before following the nurse. My kids were allowed in the prep room so they came with me. My blood pressure was over the top. The nurse smiled and said;" in this room blood pressure is always over the top – no worries, it is rather normal."

Most of what happened next was a blur. I do remember my son saying that he was really touched that these two guys came all the way out here. Yes, and they will have to walk back as well.

Then I remember nurses, then the doctor saying hello. The procedure was explained once again and then they put the meds in my IV and I was out.

The next thing that I remember was waking up and the doctor being there. He was telling me that all went well. He told me that they had to get pretty close to the heart and they wanted to keep me overnight for observation. OK by me. I was just glad it was over.

When my kids found out, they wanted to stay with me. And they did for a while, but then I told them to go home. I was tired and worn out. They wanted to stay, but I assured them that watching me sleep would not be very entertaining. I sent them home. They spoke with a nurse and left their phone numbers. If anything would change, they would be here in no time. The hospital was only a few miles from my house.

But all was well. My heart felt like it was beating differently, much harder. I talked to the doctor about that and he assured me that this is very normal. I relaxed.

My kids came to pick me up the next day. I was glad to go back home. The doctor told me to take it easy for the next few days but get back to a normal day to day routine within a week or so. It was nice to just stay home. Both of my kids spoiled me and I enjoyed that. I did skip one week of homeless ministry, but then was right back out there.

Everyone was happy to see me. They were surprised that I came back so quickly. Daniel and Paul both walked with me and helped me hand out the food. They wanted to make sure that I was not working too hard. I told them that I was fine, but they would not listen. So, I let them take care of the food, while I just chatted with everyone. I saw true worry and care in each of their eyes. Daniel told everyone about my son. "He is huge! A real Marine!" He told everyone. That particular weekend I got many more hugs from everyone than ever before. I felt so honored and so loved. Their concern for me was genuine and again I felt overwhelmed. I did not stay as long as I usually did that first weekend after my procedure, but after that, I was back to normal.

A typical meal.

This is me preparing the Christmas gifts.

This is me, I just got done feeding the people in the background.

The lady on the right is Marleea. She was bringing food and prayer.

Above: My friend Daniel and I.

Below: This was a typical meal at 'church without walls'

Marleea making announcements.

This was my cart with all the goodies. The brown bags are in the bottom and
the warm meal is packed securely in the basket.

10

M arleea

I HAD NOT GONE to Church without Walls for several weeks. Between work, my procedure and going every Sunday to the square, I just was too busy. But there was a Saturday on which I had the time and I wanted to go. On my way there I stopped at Starbucks and bought 2 travelers with about 30 cups and creamer and sugar and the works. Real deal coffee was always very much welcomed there. When I arrived, things seemed different. More tables and more people were there. I quickly was surrounded by several homeless who saw the Starbucks travelers and they came to ask if they could have

some – oh yes!! I got to chat with them for a little while. Then I made my way to the volunteer desk.

I HAVE NEVER SEEN it that busy! All kinds of homeless people surrounded it and were waiting to talk to someone. I stayed back to see what was going on, when one of the other volunteers came to talk to me. She said" there is a new sheriff in town! This woman is amazing! She has taken control of all of this." I walked away and looked for a couple of people to whom I wanted to talk. I got busy with them and then the service started. I always enjoyed the mini-sermon that was held. The pastor always had an uplifting message for the homeless. And the worship was amazing too. I saw lots of the homeless with the bibles that I had handed out and it truly warmed my heart. When the service was over, the food was handed out and I helped with that. I heard people talking about the new leadership and this wonderful woman. I wanted to meet her.

LATER I SAW that the volunteer table was clearing up and I went over there. I saw a young girl, about 18 – 20 years old, a beautiful young lady. She wore her hair very tightly to her head in a little bun in the back. She was talking to a homeless woman, and she had the most beautiful smile for her. But she was too young;

she could not be the leader everyone was talking about. I walked up to her and when she was finished speaking to the woman, she looked at me and smiled asking me how she can help me. I asked for the new leader of the ministry. Her smile got bigger; she got up, reached out her hand to me and said"That would be me, I am Marleea." I was surprised. I shook her hand. I tried not to let my surprise show, but she got me. "I am young, I know, but I love the homeless and I am a Marine. I know how to organize and that is what I am doing. It is a lot of work!" "I can help! Let me know what you need and I will help" I offered. She took me up on that right away. "Let me show you what I have here" she said as she was grabbing a big box. In that box were all kinds of papers, folders, ring-binders and other things.

S<small>HE EXPLAINED</small> that she had a list of businesses that are willing to hire homeless people. I was really surprised how very organized she was. She helped the homeless with jobs, with places to stay, had addresses where the homeless people could take showers and she had a stack of bus passes. I quickly understood why everyone talked about her and praised her leadership.

I sat down and she showed me everything she had and told me that she would really love it if I would help. I told her I would.

. . .

THE NEXT TIME I saw her was at a ministry meeting at the church. A leader there held monthly meetings with all the ministry leaders to see what everyone was up to. It was a rather generic meeting. But I learned that Marleea had all kinds of other resources for the homeless. She had a storage room where clothing was kept. Men's, women's, and kids clothes were neatly stored. She organized a clothing drive and had received a lot of donations and managed for it to be an ongoing thing. Every

Saturday we went to the storage room and got lots of bags filled with clothes.

THE CLOTHING WAS SPREAD out for the people to pick a new outfit. It was amazing. Marleea had no end of ideas. She wanted to have a house for the homeless. She was working on donations for that. Her vision was that this house would be self-sustained by the homeless. You were there only for a limited time. You needed to clean up and find work and eventually move into your own place. Then you would be required to help others do the same. Yes, I agreed with all the other people. She was truly amazing! 19 years old and a heart of pure gold! Then she mentioned just 'by the way' that she had 2 homeless people stay in her house with her and her husband and her little baby boy.

. . .

M<small>ARLEEA</small> <small>BROUGHT</small> a brand new leadership to the Saturday outreach. She connected people who needed help with things like yard work, painting and other work, with homeless people who had the skills to do the work. For a good warm meal and a few dollars, they got to work and then could get referrals for other jobs. She organized people who were cooking as well. Meals were better organized, people were given specific tasks and they followed through.

B<small>ACK</small> <small>IN</small> <small>THOSE</small> days it was, and I believe it still is, against the law to feed homeless people. Marleea took charge of that as well. She contacted the police and talked them. I am not sure how in the world she did it, but the police left us alone. It was amazing to work with her side by side and see her come up with new inventive ways of getting donations, money and new volunteers.

R<small>ICHARD</small> <small>WAS</small> one of the homeless who stayed at her house. No wonder I had not seen him in while! He was a very kind individual himself. I talked about him earlier in the book. Him being homeless himself, he helped other homeless people also. He was no longer homeless and I was so happy about that. He was in his late 50's and his body needed to rest in a warm bed and not lay on the cold hard concrete of the streets in San Diego. Marleea's heart was bigger than her entire person! She loved people, all people but she had a very soft spot in her heart for the homeless.

WE PARTNERED up with a lady who had several private homes that she shared with homeless people. She charged $10 per night but you had to pay in advance for at least one month. She also had the mindset of giving homeless people a hand up – not had hand-out. It was amazing in a just a few months this small group of women helped dozens of homeless people off the streets. Some of them would come to Church without Walls as helpers. They also were willing to speak to the homeless about how they can get off the streets if they wanted to. It made a difference not to just hear that they should get off the streets, but hear how they can achieve that. It made a big difference and motivated lots of them to try. The thing is most homeless people do not like being homeless. But once you are, it is very difficult to get back to a normal life. Even if you have clean clothes and you can go to a job interview. This possible employer will want to have your address and phone number to call you back. When you are homeless you do not have that and the moment the possible employer finds out that they are talking to a homeless person, everything changes.

There are few businesses that are willing to hire homeless people. It is so sad because all they want is a chance.

M<small>ARLEEA GOT</small> the church involved with making t-shirts for everyone, this way people would know who the helpers were. What a brilliant idea! We had to pay for them, but if someone could not pay for it, they still could have one anyway. I saw Richard again in one of the shirts, talking to other homeless people. I got one too, I still own it today.

I <small>AM TRYING</small> to find words to express how happy all this made me feel! Richard having a home, me working with Marleea, it was truly overwhelming. I spent just about every Saturday at Church without Walls. The amazing transformation of that ministry was all due to Marleea's hard work. So many homeless people were helped with food, clothing, jobs, a place to stay, prayer, God's word, counseling and so much more. Yes, Marleea made it happen that a counselor came once a month. She also organized barbers and hair dressers to volunteer on Saturdays. One of the first guys to get a free hair cut was Richard. His long ponytail fell and the beard as well. He looked like a different guy. It was so touching to see all this positive change. Marleea put the stamp of her personality on everything – and everything was better because of her.

I ₕₐD the amazing pleasure to work with Marleea for a little more than one year. During that time, she gave every free moment to the ministry. Then one day I got a phone call from one of the volunteers and she told me that Marleea passed away. - What? Marleea was 21 years old. That is not possible! She was not sick – how could she pass away. "If this is some twisted joke, it is not funny!" I said to her. But I heard her crying over the phone. She was not joking. Marleea drove a motor bike and there was an accident that killed her on the spot. Her young life- gone. The light that she brought to the ministry, the light that she brought to each person with whom she came in contact, was forever extinguished. I felt tears running down my face. I felt numb.

Iₜ ₜₒₒₖ me a couple of days to actually process the fact that she was actually gone. Marleea was dead? My heart was hurting. I looked towards the sky and yelled out loud "Why God?? Why???"

Tₕᵢₛ ₓₐₛ something that went through the homeless community, like a wildfire. There were lots of tears, and lots of grieving. She was a one of a kind. I never had met anyone like her before or after. One thing all of us knew: She was dancing with Jesus. Her work on earth was done.

THERE WAS a memorial service at the church for her. Hundreds of people were there. Many of the homeless were there as well. There was a big photo of her. With her hair tightly brushed into a bun in the back of her head. And yes, the photo captured her beautiful smile perfectly.

THINGS CHANGED VERY QUICKLY. Marleea's husband asked Richard to leave the home where he had lived for the last year with Marleea and her family. He also was a Marine and his time came to move. Richard was homeless again.

SOME OF THE volunteers from church were told by the church what to do next. They took over all the paperwork. It was never the same again. Marleea's dream of a house for the homeless was gone with her. The church did not want to pursue this because of the liability factor. Something Marleea did not care about. She just wanted to help.

. . .

I AM STILL in contact with her Mom. I am grateful for that. Marleea was an inspiration to me and so many others. She had the biggest heart, the biggest love for homeless people. I do not know any other person who worked as hard as Marleea. Her efforts helped so many in the homeless community. Whether it was food, clothing, job hunting, counseling, a place to stay or simply her beautiful smile, she will be missed! I will never forget her. I do believe that she is in heaven, helping Jesus to prepare beautiful homes for the homeless. I know in my heart that her heavenly reward is greater that I could ever describe. I love you Marleea, I will see you again!

CHAPTER Fourteen Out of work

MOST CHRISTIANS WILL GIVE money to their church. I did not. I attended a big mega church and I felt I am paying for the food that I bring to the homeless and that was my tithing. After all, tithing is money that goes to God and His work. Each weekend, I was feeding between 40 and 70 people. Depending on what I cooked and how I could transport it. I spent between $150.00 and $200.00 every weekend. That was a pretty good chunk of what I earned. But I had enough to live on and the homeless people had nothing.

WELL, it was on a Monday morning when I went to work. We always had a meeting on Mondays. The rest of the week, I was usually out with clients. This particular Monday I got to work early as always and I saw my supervisor too. I got along with him just fine. He came to my housewarming party when I first bought it. I had asked him how secure my job is because I wanted to buy a house. His response had been that I was his best consultant and I should buy that house. I did and I really loved the house. It was a bit of a fixer upper, but I had some money in savings that I used for the down-payment and then for fixing what needed fixing. I also had charged a bunch of things to my credit card; after all, I had a well paying job. I was proud enough to make that house-warming party and showed off my new home.

As I WALKED by my supervisor's door I smiled and said hello. He seemed different, but I just walked over to my little cubicle and got my paperwork ready for the meeting. Here came my boss and asked me to come to his office, he needed to talk to me. I followed him and sat across from him. He clearly was nervous, as his hands were shaking. I asked him if he was OK. I had never seen him like this before. "No" he said, "I am not OK, I have some bad news for you Petra." He did not make eye contact with me when he said "we have to lay you off". It seemed like I could hear my blood rushing through my veins. I felt heat in my face, the kind of heat when your face turns red. "What?" my voice sounded broken "what did you say?" "Petra, I am truly sorry, but the economy is not the best and we are not making the sales that we should. We have to make some changes and you are lowest in seniority." I felt my hands shaking and my voice was too when I said "but you said my job is secure? You said go ahead and buy the house. You are letting me go?" I asked. He just nodded while looking at the table. He said some other things, but honestly, I did not hear him. My thoughts were racing, I was unemployed? I never in my life lost a job before. I was not sure how to handle it. I got up and left his office and started packing my stuff. When I left I saw everyone else in the conference room. The weekly meeting was going on as if nothing happened. I got to my car and drove home. My daughter was home, she had taken a couple of days off. "Wow Mom, what are you doing home so early?" she asked. "I was let go. I no longer have a job" She laughed and said "No really, how come you are home?" I looked at her and I felt tears rolling down my cheeks. I could not speak. She now realized that I was serious. She came to hug me and she started praying out loud for me. She was asking God to comfort me and to provide for me like He always does.

S<small>HE THEN MADE</small> us coffee and we sat and talked about the future. I should apply for unemployment money – but I knew that this would not be enough to pay the mortgage. It did not take very long before I started to panic, how were we to eat? Pay bills? Pay the mortgage? Oh my goodness, what about the homeless people? I really started to cry then. I cannot feed them any longer.

I <small>REALIZED</small> I needed to pray about this and let a couple of days go by before I would make any decisions. Sadness was in my heart when I thought about the fact that I could not afford the homeless ministry any longer. But then I thought hey, I had already bought the stuff for the next weekend. I would go out there at least one more time and I would tell them about it and bring whatever food I already had. It would not be as extravagant as it usually was, but I had a sandwich and a bottle of water for each of them. Yes, that is what I will do, I thought.

. . .

THAT WAS ACTUALLY EXACTLY what I did. I parked my car at my usual parking spot at the square. Daniel was there waiting for me. He had a big smile on his face, as always. He gave me a hug and I had to fight tears. He realized right away that something was different. He looked at me and asked what was wrong. We sat down and I told him all about it. Daniel got upset. "They can't do this to you! I think you could sue them! That is not right." I smiled at him and told him that they can do that. This is part of being an 'at will' employee. We talked a little longer and then I started to walk around the square and handed out my sandwiches. I was telling the homeless that this might be the last time that I come out here for a while. They all were sad for me. Everyone promised to pray for me. I saw Daniel talking to the homeless people that I just talked to, but I did not really give that a second thought.

I WALKED around the square and wound up back at Daniel's area. Daniel and Paul were standing there and smiled at me. It was one of these big smiles that caused me to ask "What's up?" Daniel said "Petra, when you come here and you bring us food that is always really nice. But what is most important to us, is the fact that you care about us. You talk to us, you spend time with us. We would like you to come anyway. You do not have to bring food. Just come and spend time with us!" My eyes were filled with tears as he continued "you know everyone knows what happened and I talked to some of them and we collected some money for you so you can get gasoline for your car and you can come here. Please take it and come next week OK?" Tears were rolling now. How could I say no? I did not want to take the money, but he insisted. It was $28.60. It was enough to fill up my car for sure. I promised I would be back next week.

I OFTEN POSTED about my homeless ministry adventures on Facebook. I wanted to inspire other people to do something for God. I talked about the joy that I felt when I helped the homeless. I took photos of the food that I prepared. I did that to give people a visual and I always encouraged people to do something similar or mentor a child, help an elderly person or whatever God puts on their heart. Well, that day I posted something like this: I lost my job. With no income, I will no longer be able to do my homeless ministry. My heart is breaking because they will not get food. If you can help, please go and bring some food out to them or do whatever you can. Please most of all – would you pray that I will find work quickly? Thank you so much!

I DID GET a bunch of comments on my post, people said

they were sorry that I lost my job; others said they would pray for me, and things of that nature. 2 days later I had a comment from Brandon on my post. Brandon was a Facebook friend only. I had never met him or spoken to him. I honestly do not even remember how we became Facebook friends. I read his comment several times; it took a little bit for me to truly understand what he was saying. "I want to help, how can I send some money your way?" I felt my eyes fill up with tears. He wanted to help me bring food to my friends! I gave him the info he asked for and thanked him. I told him that this is a direct answer to prayer. A couple of days later I received $300.00 I was in such awe. I was hoping for $50 so I could go and bring a sandwich and water. The $300 was enough to make a couple of small meals, like spaghetti, and some juice and cookies. Brandon was doing what God had put on his heart and I told my homeless friends to start praying for this wonderful man. I am sure that they did, I know I was.

THE NEXT COUPLE of days were difficult for me. Like I said, I had never lost a job before and I just could not wrap my arms around the fact that I actually was unemployed. I really was not sure what I should do.

. . .

I_{T WAS} mid-week when I really felt panic, what if I lose the house? What if I can't find work? After all, I was in my 50's and it was not easy to find work. I decided I needed to pray. I prayed and I told God all about what happened and I told Him that I would need His help. I really do not know what to do.

W_{HEN} I _{FINISHED} my prayer and had said 'amen' the phone rang.

The call was from a client that had purchased accounting software just a couple of weeks earlier. I just said hello when I answered the phone. "Is this Petra?" was the question. "Yes" I replied. "The Petra that works with the accounting software?" was the next question. "Yes" I confirmed. "Ah perfect! This is Tom; you were there when we purchased the accounting software a couple of weeks ago. We went with your company because of you. You seemed so knowledgeable and you were so nice. We bought the software because you would implement it. This morning they sent out some guy who is supposed to do the implementation. They told us that they had to make cuts and you were it. Well, the guy is rude and bossy, and we do not want to deal with him. We were wondering if you could do the implementation and we will pay you directly." My mouth was open. I closed my eyes and said a very quick silent prayer 'God, you are amazing', then I talked to the client. They were MY clients now. I discussed how we will proceed, and I would be there the very next day and would help them with their implementation.

I CALLED my daughter and told her. "God is good" she said. Yes indeed. I never had a prayer answered that quickly! Then again, God knew how scared I was. He took care of me right there and then. He knew that I needed His help and Him comforting me. He came through for me in a mighty big way that only He knows how to do.

OF COURSE, then I started wondering if I could get in trouble. I did not ever sign a non-compete contract, so no, I did not think I could get in trouble. But I contacted my prior boss about it anyway. When I talked to him about it, to my surprise, he was very supportive. In fact, he mentioned a couple of other clients that I should call. I realized he felt bad that I lost my job. I did not ask why I really lost my job at that time. A few weeks later I found out that it really had nothing to do with me.

THE COMPANY I worked for had a silent partner, her husband's business went belly-up and she showed up and said that she needed a job. My boss told her that they were fully staffed and do not have a job. She then said: well, then make one! Make a job for me or I want my investment back. I was that casualty. I actually felt relieved when I heard that. I knew it had nothing to do with me.

T<small>HE FOLLOWING</small> weekend I was out at the square with a bunch of food. I happily told everyone what had happened. Everyone was thrilled, most of all me. I knew that all of them had been praying for me and I thanked them for their prayers. I assured them that it was because of their prayers that my situation cleared up that quickly. And my heart was happy that I was able to bring food for them as well. Yes, God had my back in a very big way.

11

Norma

MANY TIMES I was not alone when doing the ministry. My daughter came with me on a regular basis; various people who do this ministry came to join me for a couple of times. I always told anyone who ever came with me to go on a different day. That would mean instead of them receiving food on Sunday evening, they would receive food on another day as well. But don't get me wrong, I loved people who were interested in the ministry to come along. Most people have this idea of all homeless folks being either mentally ill, or drug users, drunks or simply "bums" and that is just not the case.

One of my very best friends ever is Norma. I met her in a church where I worked. We met doing ministry together. We hit it off right away. We did the ministry weekly and started to talk outside from those days. I told her about the homeless ministry and she was interested. She asked me a bunch of questions about it and one day she asked if she could come along. Yes of course! I told her for the whole experience, she should come to my house right after church. She agreed.

Usually I started the prep on Saturdays and so I did that weekend. I made a pasta salad and put it in the small individual containers in the fridge. So, when Norma came over, we started getting the bags ready. Each bag contained a bottle of water, the salad, a granola bar, a couple of hard boiled eggs, tiny salt and pepper bags, plastic fork and knifes as well as a napkin and a tract. In case you do not know what that is, it is a small pamphlet that talks about the gospel. I had Norma help me make meatballs. I usually have between 8 and 10 pounds of ground turkey. Cut up onions and put all the seasoning into it, form the meatballs and then bake them. Then when they were all ready, we put 2 meatballs with BBQ sauce in foil paper that we previously cut into squares. Those were then put into a big Styrofoam box that also was lined with foil paper to keep the food hot. Then we loaded everything in my car. The bags were put in a laundry basket, then the Styrofoam box. I had a foldable cart on which all the goodies were placed, and then we could just push the cart around and handed out the food.

When we got there, Daniel was already waiting for us. "My" parking spot was empty as always. I introduced Norma, they shook hands and I got a big hug from Daniel and from Paul as well. We handed them the food – Norma handed out the bag, and I handed out the meat. We made it around the square and fed 55 people that day. We stopped regularly and I prayed for those who asked for prayer. We talked with many. I remember it being a cooler evening and many of the homeless were already wrapped in their blankets and ready to go to sleep.

The first hour of the ministry Norma was rather quiet. She just handed out the bag and smiled, said you are welcome as the homeless people told her thank you. Then she got a little more talkative and struck up conversations as well.

We were out there for about 2 ½ hours, maybe closer to 3 hours when we were all done. We packed up the cart and said goodbye to Daniel and Paul. They said that the meatballs were amazing, which always made me smile because it made me happy when they liked my food.

Norma and I got in the car and made our way back. She was very quiet, so I asked her "how did you like it?" There was no response, I looked over to her and I saw her face wet with tears. The tears were just rolling over her face. I let her cry. A little while later she said "I did not expect this!" "Expect what" I inquired. "I did not expect them to be so nice, so much like anyone else! I did not expect them to be so warm and so humble." Her voice was breaking and new tears were running down her face. I focused on the road while I said "Yes, I know what you mean. When I first started doing this, I thought I am not made for this. I felt overwhelmed and did not feel this is for me. But I kept coming back. This is the kind of ministry that you either love or hate. There really is no in-between." She agreed and I was a little surprised when she said "I think I love it." I just smiled. Norma kept talking, she said "They are so sweet! They are so grateful! They deserve to be helped. How can I help?" I told her that she could come along again if she would like to. She said yes!

Norma came with me again. She brought supplies for them as well and we handed out the food and the supply. Then Norma asked if she could bring her daughter – well of course! Her daughter was in her mid twenties at the time and she never was exposed to homeless people to that extend. I remember her having a very similar reaction like Norma had. Norma and I lived 45 miles apart and it was quite a drive for her. Eventually I told Norma to start this on her own as well. But where she lived the homeless people had several food sources where they could get something to eat. Every now and then Norma came to help me. She developed great respect for the homeless people as well.

*D*ate with Jesus

AFTER ABOUT 6 years of doing the ministry I started to "wear out". I needed a break. I felt very negative about everything out there. One of the homeless fed the pigeons with the food I brought and it made me angry.

ANOTHER ASKED me why I do not bring crab salad for a change, but the real deal, not the cheap imitation stuff. That made me angry too.

Granted, they did not know that I was paying for all of this out of my own pocket. They thought that the church was funding this. I had told them that so that they did not feel that they owe me anything. But like I said, during this time, I just felt a lot of negativity.

THERE WERE some other things in the weeks prior that just made me mad. My attitude was simply not the same. It was not only the homeless, but even strangers on the road - I had choice words for them. This really is not like me! And I realized that something is not right with my attitude.

ANYWAY - THE NEGATIVITY kept coming and I realized it and began to cry, I felt so bad about being so negative. Taking things to God did not seem to make much of a difference. Getting ready to do homeless ministry became a chore that I did not want to do any longer. I prayed and I asked Jesus for a "date" so I could tell Him all about it. I wanted to have peace and quiet for this date. A Wednesday was the day. I asked Jesus to have a cup of tea with me in the back yard. I truly prepared for this. I was setting the chairs so one of the chairs was facing my chair and I invited Jesus to sit there with me.

A FEW YEARS AGO, my son had given me a water fountain for my back yard. I love that fountain. I had the water fountain on, providing such soothing sounds of the water splashing. When it started to get dark outside, I made tea. I poured a cup for Him and one for me.

I SAT DOWN and prayed out loud. I began to confess to Him all the negativity and all the things that are on my heart. I told Jesus about how the homeless and their innocent remarks get under my skin. I confessed that I get irritated more and more each week. I talked about my feelings when the homeless people seemingly asked for more and more. I told Him how hurtful it was when Pam calls me names and tells me I am from the devil. I told Jesus that I feel that I am not a good servant. I told Him that I feel so very useless. At one point I said to Him that I felt like garbage, literally like a piece of garbage. However, it was then when I could CLEARLY feel His presence and I could CLEARLY feel Him talk to me. He told me that I am not garbage. He told me that He loves me and that I am His precious child. I TRULY felt His presence out there in the yard. It was the most amazing thing that has happened to me in a LONG time!

TEARS WERE RUNNING over my face. I cried like I have not done in a long time! I did not want the time to end. I sat in silence just enjoying His presence! It was awesome. I also felt that He wanted me to share this with people. That is the reason why I put this in this book. I want to encourage you, if you have any kind of trouble in your life - make a date with Jesus! It will be one of the best things ever!! Ask Him to meet you, where ever you are and He will be there - He was for me.

13

Man making roses

ON ONE OF the Sundays I was feeding a lot of people! Something amazing happened to me that day. As I am handing out the food, I am walking down a fairly long street with lots of homeless people, just lined up. There was a little unrest amongst them. Some were arguing, just yelling out loud. I handed out the soup and the brown bag with other goodies. Immediately they quieted down, thanked me and opened their "goodie bag" and began to eat. Before turning onto the next street, for some reason, I felt the strong urge to turn around. I turned and I saw about 25 people just sitting and eating the soup that I prepared for them. The bickering had stopped, they were smiling and talking.

I FELT overwhelming love for them. I also recognized that the urge to turn around came directly from God. You know, I felt, God let me see through His eyes that day! I felt such closeness to Him!! I started to wonder - if I feel such overwhelming love for the homeless who were eating the food I made - How God must feel when He blesses us!! And I realized, although I do not have a lot of money, I am blessed with so much! I have wonderful kids and great friends. God blesses all of us with soooo much!! I asked God that day to please never let me take all His blessings for granted again. I have in the past - like most of us, taking things and kindnesses of others for granted. I am asking God today to keep my heart open - wide open - to see all the blessings much clearer. To not complain when I am in traffic - but to realize I have a car and have the privilege to drive. To not roll my eyes in long lines in the grocery store - I get to buy some groceries, not to gripe about all the taxes that are taken out of my paycheck – I am getting a paycheck - you get the point. I pray that I will keep a grateful heart through the rest of my life no matter how much or how little I have.

. . .

I THANK God that He gave me the opportunity to serve the homeless. I truly came to realize that it is a blessing to me to help them. Too few people do that. It is such a wonderful thing to do! Not to just do it - not to please others, not even to please God - just to go and see their grateful smiles. The realization that it is God Himself who called me to help the homeless is such an honor! The feeling inside is overwhelming indeed!!! God was making all of these things 'visible' to me. I believe it was a direct result from the 'date' I had with him that Wednesday before. He completely changed my attitude into gratitude.

God calls many of us into His service, but unfortunately, many ignore that call.

I FINALLY TOOK one more glance down the road and then turned around the corner. I saw Richard!! What joy! I had not seen him in a long time. We hugged and he said "Wow, you are still doing the ministry, this is great!" "Oh yes" I nodded "I sure am." He asked if he could walk with me. Gladly!! But we did not get very far. I handed out food to a man who had palm leaves all around. His long uncombed hair was all over his face. He looked up and thanked me for the food. Then he said "I can make you a rose or a cross if you want." I liked that idea. He said "OK, I will hurry up." I looked at Richard and he just nodded, grabbed my cart and walked away and handed out the rest of the food.

I LOOKED at the man assuring him "Oh take your time!" His eyes seem to get bigger and a little tear was in his eye when he said" "That is so nice of you!! Most people are in a hurry, they rush by without even acknowledging the fact that I am here. Others want to just shoo me away. But you, you tell me I can take my time. That is so very nice of you!" I smiled at him and sat down with him. I watched him using the palm leaves, making a rose. His skinny fingers were fast and talented. It took only a minute to make the rose. Then he proceeded to make a cross for me as well. Both were absolutely beautiful. We talked a little bit while he started to eat the food I brought. I asked him about the palm leaves. He told me that he makes lots of roses and crosses using the leaves and then he gives them to people.

HE EXPLAINED that some folks give him some change for the roses and he is grateful for every little bit. "I am sorry" I said" I do not have any money with me!!" He shook his head and smiled "you gave me food and you gave me something priceless today, you gave me company!" I thanked him for his kind words. He was well spoken, and I almost wanted to ask him why he is on the streets. But I have made it a habit not to ask any questions. Most homeless are eagerly chatting away, but the reasons why they are on the street was one subject only few of them wanted to talk about.

I saw Richard coming back. I said goodbye to my new friend and thanked the man for my rose and my cross. I got up and walked with Richard. "Thank you for doing this for me!" I told him with gratefulness. He made it possible for me to talk to the man who made roses for a little while. Richard just nodded and smiled. "Like old times my friend" he said. Then I asked him how he was doing. His face seemed to darken just a little bit. He looked down and said" Since Marleea is gone, nothing is the same. I am back on the street. It is hard times. But God is good." My heart was hurting for him.

There was part of me that wanted to offer him a room in my house – but where do I stop? How could I pick? There are so many homeless people in the streets of San Diego. How could I just pick one of them? Why not Daniel? Paul? Dee? Betty or Rubin? Instead, I was quiet. We walked side by side without talking. As we came to my car, Richard grabbed the final soup and brown bag. We hugged and said goodbye.

. . .

As I was driving home, I felt so helpless. I wished I could do more for Richard and more for all the others.

14

---

*D*angerous people

ONE OF THE next weekends when I got out to the square, Daniel seemed to be different. As I parked, he came to me and offered his help getting things out of my car. "Yes, please and thank you" I smiled. He came a little closer and warned me "Petra, look over my shoulder, do you see the group of people on the other side of the street?" I looked and saw about 8 – 10 men across the street. They were sitting on the street and were listening to some radio or maybe it was a CD. The music was blasting loudly and they were quietly listening, bopping their heads to the rhythm of the music. "Yes" I responded, looking at him again. "Petra, do not go to them! They are dangerous! They have drugs there and have been harassing people as they were walking by." I looked over to them again and they did not seem dangerous to me. "Thanks Daniel, I appreciate that". I had the strong feeling that God wanted me over there. I looked at Daniel and declared "You know, I think they may just be hungry too. I will take my chances. You can say a little prayer for me please." His face looked worried but he nodded, sat down, folded his hands together and silently prayed for me.

I TOOK off to go across the street. I also said a little prayer, felt God's presence very strongly and just knew that I would be OK.

As I WALKED TOWARD THEM, they all looked at me. One of them jumped on his feet and walked toward me. He was tall, about 6'5" I was guessing. He came rather close to me "hey what do you want here?" he yelled. For a split second I heard Daniel saying "Petra, do not go to them! They are dangerous!" But there was a louder voice – 'offer them food'! I looked up and asked "I was wondering if you are hungry?" He stepped back and asked "what do you have? And how much is it?" "There is BBQ chicken with potato salad, some apple juice, a granola bar and a banana, and there is no charge." I explained, grabbed a bag and handed it to him. "What are you? One of them church freaks?" he laughed and all the others were laughing too. "Well, I am not sent by a church and no, I am not a freak, but Jesus is important to me." I exclaimed, stretching my arm out more so he would grab the bag. Instead, he came closer. His face was only inches from mine and he was just looking at me. I held my head high and looked him in the eyes, just smiling at him. My heart was beating a little faster.

I was not sure what would happen next, but I was sure that God would protect me. "Yeah," he mumbled, "I think I see that Jesus thing in your eyes"

To be honest, I did not expect that, but I was so happy to hear him say that. In fact, to this day I think it was one of the nicest things anyone had ever said to me. I took a deep breath, said a small 'thank you God' in my head before reaching again to offer the bag. This time he took it. I also gave him a couple of chicken pieces which were wrapped in foil paper. I provided the same to the rest of the guys. They all thanked me and all of a sudden they were not threatening at all. They were just like all the other folks here – homeless and hungry.

"Damn, that chicken is good!" one of them said. "Oh

thank you!" I smiled at him. "Girrrl, you know how to cook!" another one said. I just smiled. "Glad you like it!"

THEN I TURNED AROUND and made my way over back to the other side. I saw Daniel and Paul; they both were on their feet, looking over to me. I walked to them and they said "We were ready to come over there and help you. But wow, you got this thing under control Petra!" We all laughed. "Well, now we can eat our food too!" Paul laughed. Yup they could.

I WALKED over to the next street and handed out food to the other homeless. I went all around the square and still had some food left. I walked on a different street and found a few homeless people whom I gave the last few bags.

ON MY WAY back I felt exhausted. I had been out there for many hours. I decided to sit down on the curb and just rest a moment when a cop car stopped next to me. The cop rolled down his window and yelled"hey you – don't get too comfortable here! You cannot sleep on this street!" He thought I was homeless. I looked down at myself, my clothing was simple and a little dirty, I had my cart and it had a laundry basket and some cardboard that I used to keep the chicken warm. Yes, I looked like a homeless person. I smiled a big smile and said "Thanks for letting me know. I promise, I will not sleep here." I got up and went to my car and drove home.

15

Winter

I_{N THE WINTER} many states have temperatures well below zero. Not so in San Diego. The temperature in the winter is usually between mid 50's to mid 60's during the day. At night it goes between upper 40's and mid to upper 50's. These are very nice temperatures for someone like me who was used to the below zero temps in Minnesota. I could sleep with an open window on any given day. But of course, I had a warm bed and a nice warm blanket. When you live on the streets, 40's are very cold. Even 50's are cold when your body lies on the concrete sidewalks of this beautiful city. And God forbid it rains. Can you even imagine lying on the street and it rains on you? I truly cannot.

I ONCE STAYED OUTSIDE during a rainy day. Once the rain penetrates your clothes, the wind feels brutally cold. I sat in my yard and allowed myself to truly get cold to a point that my body began to shake. Then I pictured the homeless people that had no choice but to stay outside. My heart was hurting. My heart was going out to them. I went back into the house and took a hot shower and put on some warm clothes and then I made my shopping list for the meal that I planned for them. For me there was no difference, I did this ministry every single weekend, whether it was cold or warm, rain or shine. Hunger does not care about the weather.

WHENEVER IT WAS COOLER, I usually made some sort of soup, chicken noodle, bean soup, chili or something like that, along with juice, a piece of fruit, a granola bar and maybe a couple of cookies for each of my homeless friends. Aside from the usual food, I picked up some raincoats at the dollar store when rain was in the forecast. These things really help out a lot. Not too far from my house was a thrift store that had very reasonable prices, I also went there and bought some sweaters. The homeless people are so very grateful for anything I brought them. One thing though, when it was clothing, they preferred dark colors. Colors like red, white, yellow simply stood out too much. I always went for the dark blue, black, grey and brown tones.

WHEN I ARRIVED at the square, it was not raining for the time being and I had time to hand out my hot soup. Something warm was always appreciated. I was going my usual route and handed out food when I saw a woman that I had never seen there before. She was in her late 30s, she was dirty and her hair was uncombed. She pushed a cart in front of her with her belongings. The clothes she wore were dirty as well. She had on several layers of blouses and sweaters, torn jeans and she was barefoot. Her face looked so very sad.

I APPROACHED her and asked her if she was hungry. Yes, she was. Her eyes got big when I handed her the hot soup and the brown bag with the other goodies. She grabbed my hand and kissed it. Tears were running over her face when she said "Thank you, thank you, thank you. You are a princess I love you." I smiled and told her she was welcome. I asked her about shoes. Her face turned sad again in an instant. "Too long of a story, you don't have time for me" she mumbled. Well, that was just not so. She had already sat down and began eating her soup. I asked if I could sit with her. "Yes princess, you can sit with me." She replied. Then she jumped up and started digging through her stuff. She found a tiny shell and handed it to me. "This is for you, thank you for the food and then you for talking to me" she said. I smiled and took it. "Thank you so much, it really means a lot to me." I told her. She ate her soup and I just sat next to her in silence. Then she turned to me and said "princess, you are nice." I smiled again, telling her "I am not a princess, just a friend. My name is Petra." She smiled "OK Princess Petra." Now I had to laugh. I told her just calling me Petra would be fine. Then I asked her if she would like to have shoes and what her shoe size is. She looked at me and her green eyes were just sparkling. "Yes, I need shoes Princes Petra" then her face turned sad and she looked on the ground when she began to tell me

"It was a week or two weeks ago. Some people came and took my shoes. They hurt me. The men hurt me. They do what they want to women here. Then they took my shoes and some other things. I had a jacket, it was warm, I had socks too. Now all I have are my shells, and these things." She pointed at the cart. I saw a pot, a couple of plastic containers, a few empty soda cans and old papers. It looked to me that most of the things she had in the cart seemed more like trash than anything else, but that was all she had. I had a hard time not to start crying. She told me that she was raped on a regular basis. Her speech was unfocused, jumping from one subject to another, to then come back to subjects she had started before. She was telling me how bad she had been treated. She told me her name was Edith. "Edith, what is your shoe size?" I wanted to know. "Nine" she said.

I TOLD her about Church without Walls. I told her that she can get food there and other supplies. I gave her the address and I said to her that I would bring her a pair of shoes. She just wrapped her arms around me and hugged me, swaying back and forward while holding on to me "You are a real princess, princess Petra. Thank you." I just laughed. I hoped that she would be there on Saturday. I handed her one of the sweaters and a raincoat and then I got up and continued walking the square.

BECAUSE OF THE fact that rain was in the forecast, there were fewer homeless people at the square. I ventured out into a new street where I usually did not go, but I knew I would find homeless people there as well. I saw a group of younger people. They were homeless as well. I was wondering how come they were homeless. But I do know that there are all kinds of circumstances in which people lose their home. They had a dog with them as well, a beautiful pit-bull. The dog sniffed me and he could smell the food. His tail was wagging. As I handed out my soups to them I said "I am sorry I do not have anything for the pooch." One of the guys responded "Like you really give a damn?" "Yes, I actually do care." I stated. I genuinely felt sorry that the dog had nothing. It was something that I added to my list of things to get for the next time. I only had a few meals left and I handed them all out, all but one.

So, I continued around the next corner. I saw a man there who was clearly homeless. He only wore pants. He was dancing. There was no music, but he was dancing and singing. I did not know the song. It sounded like something he was making up as he was singing. He was older, I would guess around 60 years old. His hair was long and he had a beard as well. There was lots of gray in his otherwise dark brown hair and beard. He had a duffle bag sitting in the corner and a couple of bottles of water. I saw an empty bag of chips and an empty bottle of beer on the floor. I was not sure whether or not I should go there, but my feet seemed to know. I felt myself walking toward him. He saw me and stopped dancing.

"Hi, how are you, would you care for some soup?" I

asked him. His response surprised me a bit"Petra, you must be Petra!" he exclaimed. "Yes, that's me" I told him, holding the food out to him. He came closer and grabbed the food. "Thank you. I heard a lot about you!" he told me. I smiled and said; "well I hope that is a good thing." He just smiled. "Are you not cold?" I asked him. "Freezing!" he said and laughed out loud. "Some jack-ass stole my other bag. All my clothes are gone. But I am dancing so I can stay warm!" He smiled a big smile. He only had about three teeth, but he smiled that big smile. "Well, I think I can help" I said as I was grabbing the 2 sweaters that I had left. I handed both of them to him. He looked at me in disbelief. He grabbed the sweaters and put both of them on right away. They fit like they were made for him. "People are right about you!" he said, "You do bring things we need" That made me smile. I replied " Yes, I try, but God really knew where I needed to go today to find you. I only had that one soup left and the two sweaters that clearly you really need." He came and put his arm around me and looked in my eyes. "Yes, now it all makes sense. You are one of His children" he said to me. He told me his name is Joe. Most people call him crazy Joe. When he told me that, I remembered that someone indeed had talked about "crazy Joe" before. They had told me about him, told me that was dangerous. He did not seem dangerous to me. But just to be sure, I told him that my husband is with me and I need to go back. "OK thank you Petra, I got to meet you, that was nice." He said and smiled.

I TURNED AROUND and walked away. Wow what a day. As I got to the corner, I turned around to take another look. Crazy Joe was sitting on the street, eating his soup. I smiled and turned the corner. I walked back to the square and to my car. I saw Edith on the other side of the square. My heart was heavy. I wanted to help her so badly.

WHEN I GOT HOME that day I went in my bedroom and I got on my knees. I wanted to pray for Edith. I could not. I did not know what to say. I usually know exactly how to pray for people. This situation with Edith – I did not have words. No word seemed adequate. I was kneeling in front of my bed and felt great frustration. Finally, I said" God, help her! God, help her! Help her. Help her. Help her." I could not even cry, I felt so frustrated and so sad for her. I do not remember how long I sat and kept saying the same thing. "Help her God help her".

THEN I FINALLY GOT UP AND took a shower. When I was done, my daughter had just come home and I told her about my day out there and I told her about Edith. My daughter reminded me that her shoe size is also size nine and she went in her room to find a pair of her tennis shoes. I took those shoes with me to Church without Walls the following Saturday. But I did not see Edith there. I did talk to one of the homeless about Edith. He told me"I know Edith! I will make sure that she gets the shoes". He took the shoes from me. For a split second I wondered if Edith will ever see the shoes, but I remembered that it is God who is in control. I let go of the shoes and he stuffed them in his backpack.

ABOUT A WEEK later when I came home from work, my daughter opened the door for me with a big smile on her face. "Edith got the shoes!" she told me. "How do you know?" I wanted to know. "Well, I was downtown today bringing some food to the homeless and I saw her!" She said. But I wanted to know "How do you know? You do not even know her." She smiled and said"I know my shoes!"

WE BOTH LAUGHED OUT LOUD. Yes she did, she knew her shoes and I had given her a description of Edith too. I never saw Edith again, but I know that God is taking care of her. God is good.

· · ·

CHAPTER TWENTY At work

I WORKED at a church in those years. And there I also ran a ministry. We called it the needs ministry, I mentioned in the beginning of this book. Anyway, I think it was because of that ministry that the receptionist forwarded a phone call from a woman in need. I answered the line, introduced myself and asked how I can help. Her story was heartbreaking "I am Silvia, I am homeless. I live in my car with my 2 cats. Everything I own is in my car. Plus, my 2 cats live in the car with me. My car stopped working and I talked to a mechanic and he said it would be $75.00 to fix it. I had $80.00 left and I said OK. But when I got there, he told me that some other stuff was broken and I would have to pay $150.00. I do not have $150.00 so this jerk is telling me that he will not release my car. My cats are in the car! My cats need food and it gets cold at night and they always snuggle up with me. I need to get into my car and he will not let me. I need help!" Her voice had gotten louder and louder as she told me her story.

I TRIED to think of how I could help her. I did not have any money with me and the church that I worked for did not have a benevolence fund. I told her that and I finished by saying"I am so very sorry! I wish there was something I could do!" She got very angry, swore at me and hung up the phone. I felt so bad for her. Our phones had caller ID. I wrote down her number and had full intentions to call her back, but people came in my office to call me into a meeting that I almost forgot about. But on my way to the conference room I said a prayer, asking God to do something. Just do something or send someone who will help this woman.

T HE MEETING TOOK over 2 hours. I had forgotten about the woman, but when I got to my desk I saw the number that I had written down. I decided to give her a call. It was almost time for me to go home. I could go there and talk to the car dealer and hopefully would be able to help in some form. It rang a couple of times before she picked up the phone. I said "Hi, this is Petra from church, you called a couple of hours ago and I just wanted to ask where you are so I..." She interrupted me," it is you, I am so sorry for my behavior! I was just so very frustrated and you were my last hope. But you know what, something amazing happened! I was sitting out there crying and I just did not know what to do. After a while the manager came out and handed me the keys to my car and said that all is paid for. Then he told me that some woman walked in the store saying that she felt God telling her that there is someone who needs help. And at first the manager said to her no, they are not hiring right now. Then the woman said no no, I think that someone here needs my help. The manager then told her about me, saying I was the only person who needed help. She then smiled and said yes, that it is. He told her it is $150.00, and the lady paid it and left without saying her name. She must have been an angel or something. So, I got my car and my cats back and all is well. But thank you for calling me back; especially considering the way I talked to you."

My voice was breaking because I started crying as she told me that this perfect stranger listened to God's voice telling her to go and help. I wondered if my prayer, asking God to do something or send someone, had anything to do with this. But whether that was so or not, it did not matter at all. God is so good. I could not believe how amazing He is and I was happy. With a cracking voice I said "that is really amazing. I am so happy that you got your car and cats back." I invited her for dinner and she accepted. We met 30 minutes later at a Denny's nearby. Yes, she was homeless. I saw her cats and her stuff in the car. So strange to think she was so much better off than some homeless people. She had a place to sleep, away from the rain. She could drive to a safe location and lock her doors. But none-theless, she was homeless. She shared this fate with so many others. She did not tell me much about herself.

But she kept talking about the woman who paid her bill. "Why would anyone do that? Why would anyone just pay my bill?" She kept asking. I cleared my throat and said "Well, God knows His children. He hand-picked that lady to help you!" She nodded and then we both ate our food.

GOING HOME, I felt closeness to God like I rarely felt before. At this point I was convinced that my prayer had something to do with all of this and God took the time to listen to me and to answer my prayer. My daughter actually taught me about praying specifically for things. Not Just 'God bless this person'. "Why?" I asked her. She told me if you just simply ask for blessings, you will never know what blessings God poured out over this person because of your prayer – but if you pray specifically, then, when God answers your prayer, you know it was your prayer that was answered and you can praise God for that. Yes, I was thinking about my daughter's wisdom when this happened. God answered my prayer. He answered it in such a way that I knew. My heart was overflowing with gratitude to Him and I praised Him.

16

J ury Duty

I RECEIVED a card from the court nearby. I was asked to do jury duty. I was actually very excited about this. I think it is such an honor to be a juror. I cleared my schedule for a week, just in case I would be picked. I had to be there at 8 AM and I was on time. I brought my laptop. I figured I could get some work done while waiting. I worked on an agreement with a new client.

The clerk came in and called about 20 people, but my name was not among them. I kept typing. The clerk came back and called out another 20 people. They all got up and went to a courtroom where they would be jurors. This kept going on all day until about 3 PM when the rest of us, who were not called upon, were told that we could go home then and we were thanked for being there.

Most people seemed relieved, but I was disappointed. I grabbed my laptop and went to my car. I was driving in the streets of San Diego. Rush hour had not started yet, so there wasn't a lot of traffic. At a red light I looked around at all the people that were walking, standing, sitting, running and I saw a familiar face, Dee!! I rolled my window down and called out to him "Dee, hey Dee." Dee turned around and his face brightened when re recognized me. He waved at me. I pulled over. I got out of the car and I went to hug Dee. "How are you my friend?" I asked him. He smiled big and said he was doing well. "How about we grab a bite to eat?" I asked. "That would nice!" he responded. "So, where would you like to go Dee, pick a place!" There was a moment of thought before he said "MacDonald's?" "Oh Dee, how about a nicer place?" I asked. "Hmm, um, well, Wendy's?" he suggested. I smiled and said "OK, how about Applebee's?" "I have never been there before" he replied. "Well, you are in for a treat" I smiled. We got into the car and I drove us to Applebee's.

The place was pretty empty because it was really not dinner time and lunch was just over. We got a very nice table. Dee was impressed with the restaurant. We ordered food and I asked him how his stomach is doing. He told me that his stomach was so much better! I was happy to hear that and inquired about his brother. "Petra, I have a buddy with a cell phone and he allowed me to use it. I called my brother and we talked for a long time. I called him back the next day and we were talking like the years of not talking just went away." "Wow Dee that is great news! Did you tell your bother that you are homeless?" I wanted to know. "Yes, I told him and he said that I should come and stay with him. Maybe I will do that."

The waitress came and brought the food. It was delicious. We were eating and Dee talked more. He told me about a time when he and his brother were getting along and how much he loves him and misses him. Then he talked about being on the streets here in San Diego. "It is hard sometimes to be on the street. People either look away and pretend you do not exist, or they yell at you to move away or they may even try to hit you. It's all bullsh.... Um it's all a crap load. "

I saw the grin on his face. He did not want to swear in front of me. How sweet and very respectful of him, I smiled back at him. "So, what else is new?" I asked. "I am eating in a fancy restaurant" he replied and we both laughed.

It was a really nice time. We were talking about all kinds of things. I honestly do not remember all of what we talked about. I do remember Dee's face. He truly liked being at Applebee's. He could not finish his food, so they brought him a box and he was genuinely impressed that the box had the name Applebee's on it. "Now you know you are eating at a nice place when their name is on the box!" he said. I just smiled. I remember him looking happy. He was opening up to me and shared times of his younger days and also times from the streets. We spent about 2 hours in the restaurant. I asked him if I could give him a ride. He said no. We hugged and I said that I hope to see him again soon. He hugged me again "me too!" he said with a big smile. Then he said "will you pray some more?" I felt very happy that this is what he asked me to do. I prayed for him. I asked for protection and for people that will not ignore him but will be nice to him. I asked God to truly bless him. I also prayed for God to keep him healthy and well. I got another big hug before I got into my car. As I drove off, I waved to him and Dee stretched out his hand way up high and waved back with a big smile on his face.

This many years ago, I still see him standing there with his hand stretched way high. I still remember his big smile. I never saw him again. I prayed for him often, counting on God to take care of him.

17

Lady in the wheelchair

Often when I came to the square, there were new people there. Homeless folks came and went. But there was always a large group of people that I had spoken to before. Lots of them knew me and were glad to see me. I walked and handed them food, then talked a little and prayed for many of them. I loved this!

One day when I came with my food, there were a bunch of new people there. I remember that day very specifically because of one lady. She was in her mid 70's and she was in a wheelchair. My heart went out to her when I saw her. She should not be on the street – was the first thing I thought when I saw her. I approached her and offered food to her. She just shook her head no. I asked her if she was sure. A man sitting close to her got up and spoke to me "my mom and I do not need the food you people have. Go away!" I just said sorry and walked to the next homeless person and handed food to him. Walked to the next one and I stood there and chatted with him for a while. In the back of my mind I kept thinking about this mother/son pair. All of a sudden, I found myself being very judgmental. The son looked strong and looked to be in his 50's. Why was he not working? Why is he not taking care of his mom? I realized that I did not know their story; I realized that I should not judge, but the face of this lady! There was so much pain, so much pain. I wanted to do something. I looked back and saw the son talk to her. No, I could not go back. He told me that he did not want the food I had. I continued handing out food to the other people who gladly took the food I offered.

As I was almost at the end of the square, I saw the son come my way. "Ma'am, I am sorry if I was rude. Some of the other folks told me that you have good food and I was wondering if I could have some of that for my mom and me?" "Yes, let me walk back with you" I replied.

· · ·

WE WALKED BACK and I was so happy that I still had some meals left over. When we got to the mom in her wheelchair, I handed her and her son food. It was a cooler day and I had a chicken noodle soup, a roll with butter, an orange and some juice. She spoke "thank you so much, I am sorry for refusing your food. But last week there was someone here handing out food and we ate it and it was old and bad. I got sick but I do not have health insurance and cannot go to a doctor. I was sick for 5 days. I just got a little better. So, thank you." I was saddened by what I heard. I assured her that my food is fresh and will not make her sick. She looked at the food and her face lit up. "Chicken noodle soup! How nice, that is so nice of you! Thank you!" She began to eat. I stayed and watched her for a little while. Then we talked as well. Her name was Lana. Lana told me that she does receive a social security check for $520 per month. Of course, that is not enough to have a place in San Diego or anywhere really. She told me that once a month they go to a hotel for a night where she washes her clothes and gets a shower.

I WAS LISTENING to her and oh my, I felt so sad for her. I told her that I have a spare room. I offered her that she could come with me if she likes. "What about my son?" was her concern "Well, he looks like a strong man who can get a job." I said and regretted it that very moment.

But of course, it was too late. She looked down on to her knees and thanked me but said she would not leave him alone. For a split second I thought maybe it would be OK to have him come too – but no, I let that thought go right away. I thought I would offer next week again, but only her. Lana and I talked a little more and then I went to hand out the remaining meals that I had left, and I drove home.

At home I told my daughter about Lana. She agreed with me, Lana could come and stay with us, but not the man. It would have been different if I had a husband, a man in the house. But it was just my daughter and me, so the decision was easy. Lana yes, but not her son.

I was excited to see Lana again and tell her about my place – but the next weekend when I got there, Lana and her son were not there. I never saw the two again. This was the one and only time when I seriously entertained the thought of bringing a homeless person to my house to live with us. God had different plans. I trust that this was best for everyone.

18

Christmas

I~N~ G~ERMANY~ C~HRISTMAS~ is celebrated on the 24th of December. The 25th is just the day after Christmas. My kids and I always celebrated Christmas on the 24th of December. On the 25th my daughter and I went to visit the homeless. That was always very special, because on Christmas, people were at home and celebrated with their families. The homeless may get a meal early in the day but then all shelters and soup-kitchens close because people want to celebrate Christmas. My daughter and I did this ministry every year, but I will just describe one Christmas. It was the Christmas after my heart procedure. For the first time in all the years that I went out there, my son said he would come as well. It felt like my heart was doing a little joyful dance. I was really excited that he would come along. My daughter came with me often and every Christmas because we always made it very special and I needed the help. But my son always said "this is not for me" and I respected that. Homeless ministry is not everybody's 'cup of tea'. But this year would be extra special because he planned to come along.

Throughout the years, the homeless people have shared a lot of their stories with me. And I talked about my life to them as well. I am proud of both of my kids and will talk about them for hours if you let me. There is a lot to brag about – yes, I am a proud Mom!

Most of the homeless folks, who were there on a regular basis, had met my daughter and knew about my son. The times he was deployed, the times I worried about him, the times when he came back from combat, the times I prayed for him. Yes, I shared that with my homeless friends. They wanted to meet him and now this would happen, yes, I was very excited!

Shopping and preparations for the Christmas ministry was always intense. We did not just bring food, but we had presents too. The presents were essentials, but still a present. Usually each package contained things like socks, soap, deodorant, shaving supplies, a toothbrush, toothpaste, and things of that nature. I also went to a second-hand store and picked up a bunch of sweaters, pullovers, blankets and sleeping bags. My daughter handwrote 60 Christmas cards. 60 was the number of people who we wanted to serve food and have presents for each of them as well. It took several days to prepare for this. Buying all the things, wrapping the gifts, separating the presents for men and women was a lot of work. Women got lady shavers and feminine products in their gift. We had 40 gifts for men and 20 for ladies. It worked out perfectly!! God is in the details!

I also made a special dinner for them. Ham and mixed fresh veggies with mashed potatoes and gravy, a piece of pie and juice.

We took my son's truck because we had so much stuff. As we were driving through the city, the streets were pretty much empty. People were home with their families celebrating Christmas. There was hardly any traffic. It was 6 PM when we arrived at the square. Somehow it was sad to me to see them on the street. I knew that they were always there, but on Christmas? It just hit me harder than it normally did. Everything was pretty still.

When we got there Daniel did not want to let us park there until he saw that I was in the truck. Daniel and Paul were both there and they were excited to see my son and my daughter with me. They were the only two homeless people that had met my son when they came to visit me in the hospital the day of my heart procedure. They were the first to get their meal and presents as well as a card. They were touched deeply by the love. Big hugs were given to all of us.

We walked around the square and the words "wow, this is Jesse?" were said by many. Jesse helped hand out the food and presents. More than one person had tears in their eyes. Food and presents that were not expected, but they loved it.

One guy that I had never seen before came towards us and asked if it is true that we have food. Yes, we did. We handed him the food and one of the presents. He froze and looked at us. "A present, for me?" he asked. "Yes, just for you, may God bless you!" I replied. His hands were shaking when he took the present and tears were running over his face. His voice was broken when he stated "It has been more than 15 years that someone gave me a present! Thank you so much!" I hugged him and wished him merry Christmas. He hugged me back, hard!

There were many tears that Christmas and many little conversations and many prayers. When it was time to go back home, we said goodbye and merry Christmas to Daniel and Paul and drove off. I turned and looked back. I saw them sitting, talking and waving as we drove by. I whispered "Merry Christmas!"

We were quiet for a while and then I asked my son "well, how did you like this?" He cleared his throat and said "Very humbling!" I smiled as he continued "I did not expect them to be so nice. It is so sad that they are on the street like that. But Mom, I understand now why you are doing this!"

We drove home in silence.

 nd now

I GOT OLDER and my body did not do so well with all the heavy lifting and bending and pushing a heavy cart. I knew that I had to stop doing the homeless ministry, but I continued for a while anyway. But then came a day when I bought a house in a small town in the Mojave Desert. I left San Diego and my homeless friends behind. I know of two people who still work in this ministry. Whenever I can, I support them with some money. My move to the desert was in 2013 and I love where I live.

There were many people that were special, too many to mention all of them. But I want to mention

David again. David had been in jail and was homeless when he was released. He worked hard on any small job he could. He is now off the streets, has a small apartment and lives a humble life. If you ask him how he did it – he will tell you "It was God who had all the work. I am just along for the ride." I am so proud of him!

I am still in contact with Brandon. He still is my Facebook friend and I asked for his permission to use his real name. Brandon is still a big inspiration to me. Not a lot of people are willing to help the homeless. He never knew me but trusted me with his money when I was out of work. I was able to feed the homeless for three weeks with this money. After that, I had work again and could finance it myself.

I am still in contact with Marleea's Mom. She and I talk on Facebook frequently. She misses Marleea so much. My heart goes out to her. Only the fact that we know that Marleea is with Jesus, makes her senseless death a little easier.

On a personal note, Marleea's Mom asked me to share how Marleea's name was chosen. I am glad to do that. Marsha and her husband Lee talked about having kids and they decided if they had a girl, they would mix their names to make a name for their daughter - Marleea. Marleea was born two years after her name was selected. She grew up to be one of the finest, loving, caring individuals that I ever met in my life. She was a huge inspiration to me in many ways, but especially when it came to homeless ministry. When I met her, she was decades younger than me, yet, her love for Jesus and her commitment to the homeless people taught me how to love them more, how to respect them deeper and she showed me what it meant to be a selfless person and to freely love other people and give your heart to them. Marleea, I miss you so much!

I MISS doing my homeless ministry!!! I love serving people. If you can help someone that is in need - PLEASE do so!! It will make you feel good, I promise! And if you are wondering why, let me tell you what I learned from my pastor:

Pastor David in my church preached on Talents just yesterday, God gives each of us talents, they are spiritual gifts. And God wants us to use them. This made me think of the homeless ministry. I sincerely hope and pray that I made God proud. For over 10 years I brought my homeless friends food, prayer and friendship. I miss those times. He also taught me that we are eternal beings and what we do with our time; treasure and talents will make an eternal difference.

I still am involved in ministry – just a different kind.

I hope that this book inspires you to step up and use the talents that God gave to you. Go out and do something for God. There is much work to be done.

inally

L<small>AST</small> <small>MONTH</small> I went to a local Wal-Mart; there was a man in front of it, holding up a sign that he will work for food. I went to the store, got what I came for, and then picked up a sandwich, an orange and a bottle of water. On my way out, I handed it to the man. I told him that I am retired and wish I could do more. I saw tears in his eyes when he said "Thank so you much Ma'am, may God bless you." I shook his hand and told him may God bless him too. This reminded me very much of the very first homeless man I ever spoke to - it was a powerful moment.

Made in the USA
Columbia, SC
27 September 2020